Millennial Millionaire

Optimize Your Financial Life and Get Rich

Blake Konrardy

Copyright © 2020 by Blake Konrardy

All rights reserved. No part of this book may be reproduced or used in any manner without written permission of the copyright owner except for the use of quotations in a book review. For more information, contact info@millennialmillionairebook.com

ISBN: 9798675973255 (paperback)

This publication is designed to provide general information regarding the subject matter covered. It is not intended to serve as legal, tax, or other financial advice related to individual situations.

CONTENTS

Foreword by Taylor Larimore — v
Introduction: meet the millennial millionaire — vii

Section I	**Maximize your income**	1
Chapter 1	Optimize your day job	3
	Do what you're paid to do	5
	Let your ambition show	10
	Ask for raises and promotions	12
	Make the most of it	19
	How I did it	23
Chapter 2	Strategically switch companies for higher pay	27
	Do the prep work	32
	Find the right job	40
	Negotiate fiercely	44
	Consider new geographies and careers	49
	Practice makes perfect	56
	How I did it	57
Chapter 3	Find a lucrative side hustle	62
	Find the right one	68
	Make it profitable	70
	How I did it	73
Section II	**Play good defense**	79
Chapter 4	Reduce expenses	81
	With or without a budget	83
	Housing	88
	Transportation	98
	Food and drink	100

	Childcare and education	103
	Debt, credit cards, and other expenses	105
	How I did it	113
Chapter 5	Protect your assets	116
	Protect your health – your human capital	116
	Protect your wealth with insurance	120
Section III	**Make your money work for you**	127
Chapter 6	Set your investment strategy	129
	Set your desired asset allocation	133
	Put your money in the right spot	140
Chapter 7	Invest in the market	150
	Use low-cost passive index funds	152
	Do it yourself	156
	Minimize tax liability	160
	Stay the course	164
	How I did it	168
Section IV	**Reap the rewards**	173
Chapter 8	Savor the journey	175
Chapter 9	Achieve financial independence	181
	Calculate your number	182
	Win the game	187

Acknowledgements	191
Resources and additional reading	193

FOREWORD BY TAYLOR LARIMORE

The average millennial has a net worth of $8,000. Blake Konrardy, at 29 years old, has a net worth over $1 million.

What separates Blake from his peers is the way he optimizes every aspect of his life. Leveraging his background as a statistician, he views his decisions as a series of objective equations to solve, something that does not come naturally to most of us.

Fortunately, Blake has laid out the solutions in terms the rest of us can easily understand, showing how he achieved his goal of becoming a millionaire at an early age. It wasn't easy, he had failures, but he did it. You may also become a millionaire at an early age by following in Blake's footsteps and using his solid investment advice based on time-tested index funds espoused by John C. Bogle and the Bogleheads forum.

Taylor Larimore

"King of the Bogleheads"

Author of *The Bogleheads' Guide to Investing*,
The Bogleheads' Guide to Retirement Planning, and
The Bogleheads' Guide to the Three-Fund Portfolio

INTRODUCTION: MEET THE MILLENNIAL MILLIONAIRE

I never imagined I'd be skiing in the Swiss Alps in August while the balance in my brokerage account surpassed $600,000. For starters, I didn't know it was possible to ski in the summer. Yet here I was wrapping up my glacial skiing adventure, riding in a gondola down to Zermatt, a village nestled under the mighty Matterhorn mountain. As I was taking off a few layers of clothes to prepare for the 70-and-sunny weather at the mountain base, I thought I might as well take this chance to check my investment account balances, since I hadn't looked in a couple of weeks. I couldn't help but smile as I saw the account at $603,327 – up over $300,000 from where it had been just two years prior.

My wife, Rachel, must have noticed me grinning like an idiot, because she asked what was so funny. When I shared the good news with her, she muttered "Oh, that's cool," before returning her gaze to the incredible mountain peaks. Her reaction reminded me that money is just the tool that enables the kind of experience we were having, so I slipped my phone back into my pocket and joined her.

You may think experiences like this are reserved for the ultra-wealthy: people with family money or Fortune 500 CEOs. However, I don't fit into that mold, and, odds are, neither do you. Fortunately, it's possible to quickly become a millionaire starting from nothing. Less than two years after that ski trip, my net worth surpassed $1,000,000.

I didn't win the lottery; I didn't inherit an estate. Rather, I was able to hit that milestone by identifying *small life changes* that can make a big financial impact. And this knowledge allows me to share some good news: you don't have to work at Google and live in a van to become a millionaire. Nothing I did was that remarkable or extreme, and that is why I am writing this book. It combines the advice of dozens of experts with my own personal lessons learned to provide the average Joe's guide to become a millionaire. I will teach you the changes you can make today to rapidly accumulate wealth and live the life you desire, without luck or gimmicks.

I realize this may sound like I am touting exactly that: a "get rich quick" scheme. That's because society ingrains a skepticism of financial success in us. We learn that you're not *supposed* to be a young millionaire. You're not *supposed* to do whatever you want in life.

You're *supposed* to rack up debt to go to college and grad school, get a decent-paying job, and buy a fancy car and a big house. You're *supposed* to pay off your student loans in 10 years, pay off your mortgage in 30 years, and retire after 40 years of working with whatever little money you've saved on the side, *hoping* you're healthy enough at age 70 to actually enjoy retirement.

However, I don't like doing what you're *supposed* to do. I don't like following the prescribed path in life. That's why, when I was 25 years old, I set a goal to be a 30-year old millionaire and live the rest of my life without having to worry about money.

I began my financial journey with a whopping $232 in my bank account at age 21 and became a millionaire less than a decade later. This book will show you exactly how I did it.

With virtually no savings and no debt, my starting position of $232 was actually a luxury compared to most college graduates. It took a rare combination of factors to make this happen: I went to a state school, received substantial scholarships, graduated a semester early, and worked part-time. I recognize this is an uncommonly fortunate starting point, so don't fret if you're starting off well in the red. Most people do, and I'll show you examples of how they quickly went from a negative net worth to seven figures.

After college, I landed my first full-time job as a statistician at an insurance company. The pay was solid: a $55,000 salary in a low cost-of-living city in Central Illinois. Many of my peers took their newfound big-kid paychecks and bought new cars or rented fancy apartments. Instead, I rented a 3-bedroom house with two roommates, where we each paid $400 a month. It wasn't luxury living, but as a 22-year-old, I didn't need much luxury to enjoy playing beer pong in our unfinished basement.

At work, I strove to quickly increase my income by doing what was guaranteed to make me money: passing industry exams and submitting patents, which provided automatic salary increases and bonuses. I also made it clear to my leadership that I wanted to move up in the company and was motivated to do whatever it took. This helped me land an internal promotion into a new department, giving me a $15,000 pay bump and setting me up for higher-paying jobs in the future.

During this time, I was also experimenting with a few side gigs to earn extra income. My first was a hip-hop blog that paid some of my college apartment rent and generated an extra $5,000 when I sold it. Unfortunately, that little success inflated my ego enough that I began to believe I was an entrepreneurial prodigy, and I quickly lost that $5,000 trying to start a company making protein-fortified beer (who could have guessed that idea would flop!?). After this and a few more business duds, I had some real success in a side gig using my background as a statistician to develop a predictive model for sports betting. It turns out my most valuable skills at work were also useful at making money on the side.

At age 25, I moved to San Francisco so I could save more money. Yes, you read that right; I moved to the most expensive city in the country to increase my saving rate. There's a common misconception that high cost-of-living areas are a nightmare for accumulating wealth. While that's true if you're working a minimum wage job, if the right opportunity (and salary) can bring you there, it can actually *accelerate* your income growth. While my rent was nearly 10 times what it was in Illinois, I doubled my salary and got a significant relocation check that I pocketed and invested. Another significant event happened during this time: I married my wife, Rachel, who is financially savvy in her own right.

After growing my net worth to $500,000 in San Francisco, I recognized my solid financial footing and made a non-financial life decision. Rachel and I returned to our true home of Chicago to be closer to our family and friends. During this move, we leveraged our high San Francisco salaries to negotiate pay at our new jobs, ending up with about the same income and significantly lower expenses.

Throughout this time, I kept my expenses in check by restricting my spending to what actually made me happy rather than buying nicer stuff. Spending money is an exercise in prioritization, and I prioritized travel. During my journey to $1 million net worth, I was able to visit Japan, Switzerland, Italy, Germany, Austria, France, Spain, Costa Rica, and Mexico, not to mention dozens of cities here in the U.S. I even took a weekend trip to England just to watch a Manchester City soccer match. Prioritizing my spending on travel helped me maximize my happiness while keeping my other expense categories low.

By increasing my income and maintaining low expenses, I was saving a lot of money. But I wasn't just stashing it under my mattress. Rather, I followed the advice of the late Jack Bogle, founder of renowned investment firm Vanguard, to invest in low-cost index funds and benefit from the increasing value of the stock market. Originally, I invested all my funds in a simple target retirement fund; then as I learned more about investing, I optimized my investments to reduce my expense ratio and increase my returns. My investing success was not as important as my saving rate, but it made a big difference in the three years leading up to the million-dollar milestone.

I hit $1 million net worth on December 20th, 2019, a few weeks before my 29th birthday. However, I didn't have too much time to celebrate, as my millionaire status was short-lived. The early 2020 market downturn pulled my portfolio below $850,000. Unfortunately, I am not a savant investor who can predict the future to avoid market downturns. While it certainly wasn't fun to lose hundreds of thousands of dollars in a few days, I held true to my principles, continuing to save and invest in the market, recognizing that these short-term fluctuations are insignificant to my long-term financial journey. By July of 2020, as I write this, the market has rebounded – and coupled with my increased savings, propelled my net worth past $1 million to its highest point yet.

So how did I end up in this great financial position? I figured out how to make a series of *small* changes that add up to rapid wealth accumulation. Of course, there was some luck mixed in, but none of the steps I took are that difficult to replicate once you understand the principles. And it doesn't require perfect execution, either. I made plenty of mistakes along the way. That failed protein beer company cost me $5,000 (not to mention the embarrassing amount of time I spent on it). I got too trigger-happy switching jobs and ended up at a place where I was so stressed that I quit after only nine months. But even with these mistakes, I was able to quickly become a millionaire. You can too, and I will teach you how.

The goal of this book is to help you reach $1 million net worth as soon as possible. Successfully accomplishing this goal boils down to one simple formula:

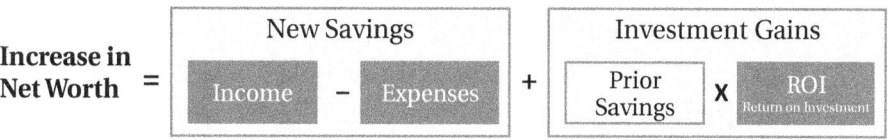

Following this formula, the increase in your net worth is equal to your new savings plus your investment gains. We can break down the amount you save further to your income minus your expenses. Then, your investment gains are equal to how much you had already saved multiplied by the rate of return you get on those savings through investing. The three highlighted factors of income, expenses, and ROI show where you can take action to accelerate your wealth accumulation.

This framework to get rich is simple. However, becoming a millionaire takes more than understanding the basics. It requires harmonious optimization of each element of the equation.

That is the core value you will receive by reading this book. Leveraging my background optimizing functions as a statistician, I will show you how to alter your everyday decisions to optimize your net worth gain. This includes the nitty-gritty detail of how to optimize your:

1. **Income** by proactively managing your career. I'll provide you the exact phrasing to successfully ask your boss for a raise. I'll demonstrate how to overcome salary anchoring to make 30% more at a new job. And I'll help you earn money on the side doing something you love.
2. **Expenses** by consciously prioritizing your spending on what makes you happy and cutting out the things that don't. I'll show you how to save thousands a year on housing, transportation, and more, without using a budget. I'll even answer the age-old question of whether you should rent or buy a home.
3. **Investments** by making smart fund selections that maximize your returns without relying on hot stock picks or finding the next bitcoin. I'll teach you how to leverage investment tax tricks that have saved me over $100,000. And I'll show you how to passively earn more money than you do in your day job, allowing you to retire and stay rich.

Before getting into these details, becoming a millionaire may still sound like a crazy fantasy. Maybe this will sound less crazy: if you're starting with nothing today, you can become a millionaire in under 20 years by saving and investing $20,000 a year.

The advice in this book will help you rapidly accumulate wealth using a combination of a little hard work and a lot of determination. These techniques work in good economic times and bad, and they don't just work for me. Here are three more millionaires from different backgrounds, all of whom discovered how to optimize the net worth equation:

- Matt started his career as an electrician straight out of high school and became a millionaire at age 30 without ever earning a six-figure salary
- John, a civil engineer, got married and had two kids before hitting $1 million at age 31, enabling more family time for him and his wife
- Lindsey graduated law school with $280,000 in debt before earning her way to $1.3 million net worth 8 years later

These three independently discovered how to optimize their income, expenses, and investments. By analyzing their experiences, combined with my own, I will provide you with a clear path to riches, regardless of your education level, career field, or financial starting point.

So don't fret if your goal to become a millionaire feels a million miles away. Instead, let's focus on the path ahead and dive into the step-by-step process to make you a millionaire.

SECTION I

Maximize your income

You'll recall the net worth formula I shared in the introduction:

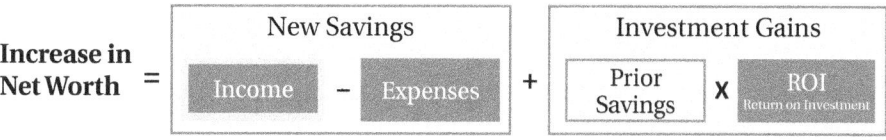

This initial section of the book will focus on the first component of that formula: income. And we'll start with the area where you can make the most immediate impact: your current job.

CHAPTER 1

Optimize your day job

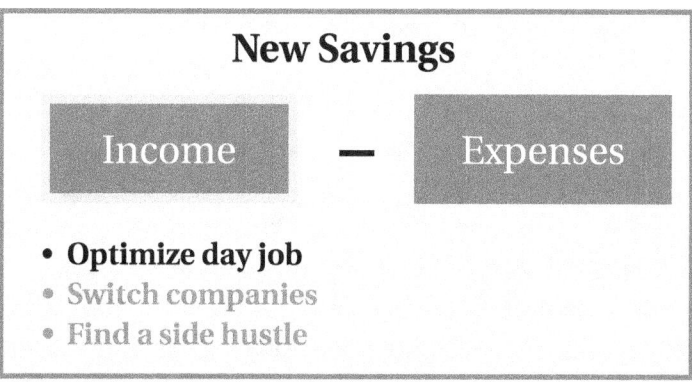

Maximizing your income is hands-down the best thing you can do for your finances. Unfortunately, it's also the most frequently ignored. Finance literature and media place an undue significance on investing, the "sexiest" aspect of personal finance. It makes sense; investing appeals to the crowd looking to get rich quick without doing work. It's fun and exciting when it's treated like gambling. You can listen to the financial talking heads and bet on Tesla stock to drop just like you can go to the casino and bet it all on black.

However, this book isn't about achieving that gambling high. It's about making you rich. While investing is important, it doesn't do anything for you until you've already built up a sizeable portfolio by saving. If you earn incredible investment returns of 50% on your $10 portfolio, congratulations – in just 12 short years you'll be a thousandaire.

Instead, you can become a millionaire in that timeframe. But to do so, you'll need to save more money, and the best way to do that is to increase income. Increasing income should be your top priority because, unlike cutting expenses, it has unlimited financial upside. There is only so much you can do to reduce your spending, but there is always a way you can earn more money.

Let's say you make $70,000 a year and have a 30-year mortgage on a $300,000 house. You want to accumulate wealth and retire early, so you're looking for a way to increase your saving rate. One extreme option is to sell your house, eliminate your mortgage payment, and live rent-free in your van in your company's parking lot. Alternatively, you could touch up your resume and find a new job for a 20% salary increase. Both options give you the same amount of additional cash to save. Now, I'm not judging you if you chose the van option – in fact, I know someone who did. But in my opinion, getting the 20% salary increase is much easier, more fun, and less stinky.

This example makes the power of increasing income clear, and you have this power right now. It just takes some focus and optimization to leverage that power and start rapidly accumulating wealth.

To do that, we'll take cues from professional income optimizers: business owners. You must take control of your career and manage it like you would manage a business. This means intentionally making decisions based on what's best for you, not what's best for the company you happen to be working for at the time. Rather than just showing up to work and getting the job done, you need to market your services and constantly look for opportunities to increase your personal revenue. You need to become a business. Jay-Z said it perfectly with his lyric: "I'm not a businessman; I'm a business, man."

Optimizing your income means doing more than just working hard. It means understanding the job market and effectively playing the game. After adopting this mentality, you can dramatically increase your income, starting with your current day job. This chapter describes tactics for increasing pay at your current company, which will also improve your ability to switch companies for an even greater salary increase.

The goal of any for-profit company is to increase shareholder value, which generally means maximizing profit. Maximizing profit, in turn, means they want to pay you as an employee as little as possible to keep performing your job. This isn't some "corporations are evil" conspiracy; it's a core principle of capitalism. Companies seek as high of a profit margin as possible, and your salary is an expense that eats into that profit margin. This is true even outside of corporations. Take teachers, for example; the school's goal is to provide as good of an education as possible with the money available from taxes, meaning it does not want to pay more than it absolutely needs to for teachers.

As a result, your employer's goal to maximize its profit and your goal to maximize your personal profit are in direct conflict. Because of this, raises and other opportunities for salary increases likely aren't going to present themselves organically. You must seek them out.

Do what you're paid to do

Assuming you're like most people, your primary reason for working is to make money. This motivation should be the underpinning of everything you do at work, including where you focus your time and energy. Following this mindset, the first step to increase pay in your current job is to do what you're paid to do. That may sound obvious, but **by maximizing your variable compensation, you can increase your earnings by 30% or more** without getting a raise or promotion.

Most employees have some form of variable pay included in their total compensation package, including hourly wages, commissions, or an annual bonus. To optimize this variable pay, you first need to know which of these opportunities are available to you. Start by creating a list of ways you can earn additional income outside your base salary at your current job. This may require some digging, as HR usually doesn't share a list of "ways to make more money."

To help create that list, here are some common variable components of compensation; you can check if these are available in your current job:

- Hourly pay and overtime
- Commissions paid as a percentage of sales or revenue attributed to you
- Annual performance bonuses, often expressed as a percentage of your base salary
- Automatic salary increases for educational milestones like degrees or certifications
- Ad-hoc bonuses
    - New hire referral bonuses for referring a new employee to the company
    - Achievement awards for successfully completing projects or providing excellent service
    - Intellectual property bonuses for creating inventions and patents

It's likely you will miss a few opportunities when you first create this list, which is okay. One way to keep it updated is to note any time a coworker is recognized for an accomplishment and determine whether there was a financial benefit associated with it. It also helps to find someone else at the company with a similar income-focused mindset with whom you can compare notes. How can you identify others who share this mindset? A good place to start is to check whether they have read or would be interested in reading this book. If so, you can discuss which aspects apply to your company.

This list you have created forms the basis of your personal compensation scorecard, which you can use to assess how well you are optimizing your income in your current job. After identifying each opportunity for additional pay, the next item to add to your scorecard is a reasonable amount you could earn if you focused solely on maximizing that component. For example, if your annual bonus target is 5% of your $60,000 salary and top performers can earn 150% of target, the maximum amount for your annual bonus is $4,500. Determine this max reasonable value for each component and add up the total to calculate your total possible additional income in your current job. Then, enter your actual earnings from the last year to determine how well you're doing.

Included below is a sample scorecard for Rick, a software engineer at a large consulting firm. His base salary is $80,000, and he receives an annual bonus of up to 10% based on his individual performance ranking. His firm also offers bonuses for new hire referrals and patent submissions, as well as an automatic salary increase for earning various software certifications.

Rick's Compensation Scorecard		
Income Opportunity	Max Reasonable Amount	Last Year Earnings
Performance Bonus	$8,000	$6,000
Referral Bonus	$4,000	$0
Invention Bonus	$7,500	$0
AWS Certificate Increase	$10,000	$0
Total Extra Income	$29,500	$6,000

Rick determined he could earn his maximum performance bonus, refer two new hires at $2,000 each, and get three invention ideas approved for $2,500 each. He also found a potential automatic salary increase of $10,000 if he could pass an exam and earn certification as an Amazon Web Services (AWS) Solutions Architect. Unfortunately, Rick, like many employees, was not focused on these additional income opportunities during the prior year and earned 75% of his performance bonus, without any other bonuses. In total, he earned only 20% of the extra $29,500 of income available to him.

Once you have a clear picture of what's possible combined with your past results, you're ready to set a goal for the next year and develop a plan of attack. While each component of variable income requires different techniques to maximize, there are a few tips that will lead to improvements across the board.

    The first is to focus your energy at work on the things that will increase your income, which, as you'll recall, is not necessarily what is best for your company. For example, Jody is in jewelry sales and earns most of her pay through sales commission. The company that she works for sets a maximum cap on the commission that can be earned each month. She's a great salesperson, so as she approaches this cap near the end of the month, she will subtly tell customers about some new pieces they have coming in soon and that they should wait and compare before buying anything. This pushes some of her sales to the next month, helping ensure she can maximize her commission again. Is this technique good for her employer? No. But Jody is simply working within the compensation structure they set up to optimize her own finances. A smart employer will recognize when conflicts like this happen and remove the cap. Until then, Jody should keep doing whatever she can to maximize her pay.

    It is also important to recognize that you are not paid based on how much value you add to the company. Rather, you are paid based on how much value your boss and other leadership *think* you add to the company. That means to maximize your pay, you need to convince your boss and other company leadership that you are successful. To do this, you must clarify your boss's success criteria for your role. For a finance analyst, for example, this might be generating accurate reports on time and contributing analysis and recommendations to special projects. If you get these precise details in writing from your boss, you now know the two things you should focus on in your job that you can highlight during your next performance review to maximize your bonus payout.

    A final tip to maximize your variable income is to give everything a try and don't assume any aspect is too difficult for you. For example, coming up with invention ideas to earn intellectual property bonuses sounds daunting. You may consider it out of reach unless you're a genius scientist, which is what I originally thought. But not every invention needs to be Earth-shattering; often, the best ones provide incremental improvements and can be very specific to your field of expertise. As a 23-year-old with no tech or science background, I gave it a shot and asked a coworker with prior patents to walk me through the process. After learning the ropes, I submitted dozens of ideas related to car insurance for autonomous vehicles, and within a couple of years I was a credited inventor on over 20 patents (and a bit wealthier from the patent bonus payouts).

Using these tips will help you maximize performance on your variable compensation scorecard. As an example, let's look at how Rick improved year-over-year.

Rick's Compensation Scorecard			
Income Opportunity	Max Reasonable Amount	Last Year Earnings	This Year Earnings
Performance Bonus	$8,000	$6,000	$8,000
Referral Bonus	$4,000	$0	$6,000
Invention Bonus	$7,500	$0	$5,000
AWS Certificate Increase	$10,000	$0	$10,000
Total Extra Income	$29,500	$6,000	$29,000

At the start of the year, Rick met with his boss and told him that he wanted to be a top contributor and earn the highest performance ranking possible. Rick's boss was excited to hear that and agreed to outline the specific criteria he was looking for, and to give Rick monthly feedback on his progress. This helped Rick receive a top performance ranking and earn the full 10% bonus. He also took advantage of the other bonus opportunities by referring three new employees, submitting two successful invention ideas (out of his five submitted), and completing the AWS cloud computing certification. In total, **Rick earned an extra $29,000 over his base salary, essentially granting himself a 36% raise.**

By creating your compensation scorecard and focusing on what you're paid to do, you can increase your income by 30% or more.

Let your ambition show

You can complete the previous tip on maximizing your variable pay predominantly on your own, but for the rest of the income optimization tips in this chapter, you'll need to influence others to help you. This does not come easily for everyone, especially if you're naturally introverted. However, it is an important part of advancing your career. Take it from me, a self-professed introvert, that you don't need to be Dale Carnegie to win friends and influence people.

The first step in getting others to help advance your career is to make it clear what you want. You don't need to give all the details of wanting to earn enough money to retire in ten years and never return to a god-forsaken cubicle, but it's fine to let people know you want to advance. You shouldn't be afraid to say that you have ambitions much higher than your current role. Managers know that ambitious people make the best employees, even though they likely won't stick around in the same role – or even at that same company – forever.

Others at your company will want to help you, and it's not just out of altruism. Your boss, HR, and other company leaders all want to look good and feel like they're performing well too. Part of their job is to develop employees and help them grow, so most will jump at the chance to help someone who is taking the initiative to ask them about it.

To effectively start this conversation with your boss, you can share where you want to be five years down the road and ask for advice getting there. I know that initial conversation can be tough and uncomfortable; it was for me at first. But you need to have these talks if you want to advance and increase your income, and it gets much easier as you go. When I started my first job out of college, I told my boss I wanted to be a manager within five years. After hearing that, my boss immediately started giving me opportunities to lead project teams and asked me to manage the interns that summer to help build my experience. After a few more similar opportunities, I became a manager within two years of starting my career.

While your immediate supervisor is generally a good place to start, your boss can only do so much. You will need to develop your own career fan club that includes some of the most influential and powerful people in your department. To do this, you'll first need to determine who is calling the shots when it comes to promotions and raises. Oftentimes it will be your boss's boss, but it can be helpful to network diagonally with your boss's peers, especially those who are moving through the ranks themselves. You can also find a mentor outside your department, preferably in an area you wouldn't mind moving to, who can help open new opportunities that aren't directly related to your current job.

I recommend identifying 3-5 leaders who fit in one of these buckets. This will form the basis of your career advancement network. If you don't yet have a good working relationship with them, don't hesitate to reach out and say you'd like to set up a quick meeting to get their advice on your career development. That conversation could be some variant of, "Ideally over the next couple years, I'd like to prepare myself for a leadership position. I've really enjoyed that aspect working on project teams. I was hoping to get some advice from a proven leader like yourself." After that, you likely won't need to exert too much effort to maintain the relationship; a quarterly check-in is likely enough.

Starting to build your career advancement network will have planted the seed throughout the organization that you're a candidate for advancement. Your name will come up in leadership conversations, and your boss will be held accountable for helping you succeed and advance within the company. This means you will be at the front of leaders' minds when it comes to promotions and new opportunities, providing you a massive advantage over your peers, even if your performance is similar.

Another element to earning recognition is to openly applaud *others'* success. It may seem counterintuitive to praise those with whom you may be competing for promotions, but it will ultimately earn you even more praise in return. As an example of this, look at recommendations on LinkedIn. Most recommendations come as part of an exchange, where both parties recommend each other. Oftentimes this is not formalized, but there's an implicit expectation to return the favor of a positive recommendation.

This same principle holds in the workplace: recognize others' success and they will recognize yours. If you have a formal kudos or shout-out system available, leverage it frequently. In return for sending out praise to 10 coworkers, they will remember and give you credit when you earn it, likely netting you 6 or 7 rounds of applause in return. Even if you don't have a formal system, this is still useful to show leadership how well you interact with others and how highly they think of you.

By letting your ambition show, you'll build up a team of supporters who will help you advance your career.

Ask for raises and promotions

Once you've built up this career advancement network, you'll be in a great position to ask for raises and promotions. These salary increases are even better than bonuses because of their compounding impact on your income over several years. **By intentionally seeking out raises and promotions, you can add an extra $750,000 to your net worth.**

Finance media often talks about the power of compounding in the context of investing (which is amazing and will be discussed in detail later). But we don't hear as frequently about how salary increases, like investments, compound over time. You can use the "rule of 72" to estimate the long-term impact of raises. This rule states that 72 divided by your rate of return approximates how long it will take for your investment to double. In this case, your rate of return is your annual raise percentage, and your investment is your salary. For example, if you get a 7% raise every year, it will take you about 10 years to double your salary. If instead you get a 3.5% raise every year, it will take you about 20 years. Granted, it's unlikely you'll get constant 7% raises at one employer, but you can average even higher than that by getting promotions and switching companies.

To illustrate the impact of raises on your total financial well-being, let's look at an example of Juan and Mary, two paralegals who work at the same large law firm. Both have a current salary of $45,000 with expenses of $30,000 and a net worth of $0. Juan is a reliable employee with output consistently above average. However, he hates confrontation and awkward conversations, so he has not talked with his boss about compensation since he started 2 years ago. Therefore, he gets the standard company cost of living raise of 2% each year.

Mary, like Juan, is a solid employee but has built a reputation as a high performer. She does everything possible to maximize her annual raise and has negotiated increased raises with her boss. She earns an average annual raise of 4%. Neither Juan nor Mary have received promotions, so the only difference in their financial situations is the annual raise. Here is a snapshot of their finances over 20 years.

Juan: 2% Annual Raise			
Year	Salary	New Savings	Net Worth
1	$45,000	$6,000	$6,000
5	$48,709	$6,495	$35,817
10	$53,779	$7,171	$89,779
15	$59,377	$7,917	$169,580
20	$65,557	$8,741	$286,048

Mary: 4% Annual Raise			
Year	Salary	New Savings	Net Worth
1	$45,000	$6,000	$6,000
5	$52,644	$9,642	$43,996
10	$64,049	$15,386	$135,394
15	$77,925	$22,756	$301,808
20	$94,808	$32,142	$584,031

The magic of compounding is clear. In 20 years, Mary's salary is boosted to $95,000 from her 4% annual raises, while Juan's salary is only $66,000. Mary's additional income over this period allows her to save more and invest more, in turn making her even more money. This results in Mary's net worth more than doubling Juan's after 20 years.

It's clear that getting raises can have a huge positive impact on your finances. The question, then, is how to get one. Ultimately, there are two factors that influence how much a company will pay you. One factor is leadership's perception of the direct value you add to the company. For example, if you work in enterprise sales and brought in 12 new clients at $100,000 revenue with a 20% profit margin, you added $240,000 to the company's bottom line. Taking this at face value, paying you any salary below $240,000 would be a net positive for the company.

Unfortunately, reality is not that simple. Other employees contributed to that profit margin. Additionally, your company could replace you with someone else who can get the same 12 clients. That is why the second factor, your **market rate**, is more important in determining how much a company will pay you.

Covering a bit of economics 101, the market rate is the point at which supply intersects with demand. This holds true for goods and services, and your employment is a service that you are selling. In this context, supply refers to the number of people with your skillset who can do your job. For example, supply might be the pool of engineers in Boston with cloud computing expertise. Demand refers to what companies need at the time. If there is a sudden rise in the number of cloud computing experts companies need, that is an increase in demand.

The market price is where supply and demand meet – essentially, the amount companies are willing to pay to employ someone of your skillset. Of course, each individual company will have slightly different salaries they are willing to pay, and each prospective employee brings slightly different skills, resulting in deviations from the market average.

When discussing a potential raise with your employer, ensure you're armed on both fronts: the direct value you add to the company as well as your market value. You want to demonstrate the great things you've done for the company to make them more profit and justify the ask for a higher salary. To do this, create a list of your most impressive accomplishments and some measure of the company impact. You need to know the value you add and ensure your boss knows it, too.

You also want to demonstrate that your market rate is higher than what you're currently being paid. To do this, gather some intelligence on salaries using sites like Glassdoor or LinkedIn to see what your company's competitors are paying for someone of your experience. You can also reach out to recruiters in your industry to get a feel for what you might be able to earn at other companies. This will help you if you decide to get serious about switching to a new company.

When doing this research, remember that you are trying to make a point and persuade your boss that you're being paid below your worth. Ensure that your numbers tell a compelling story; if you find a competitor that pays above the market average, use that as your comparison point rather than the median on Glassdoor. This isn't the time to be conservative.

Armed with this information, create an outline of your key points and a good prediction on how the conversation with your boss will go. For example, your notes might look like the following.

- Direct company value
    - Implemented process improvements to take on workload of 2 analysts
    - Delivered analysis for joint venture, directly resulting in $5 million revenue increase

- Competitive intel
    - Median salary for senior finance analyst in our city is $15,000 higher than my current salary
    - Competitor A has a job posting starting at $20,000 higher

Let's now look at the mechanics of the ask. The best time to ask for a raise is when your perceived value at the company is high. This can happen after you deliver on a big project or if you've recently taken on more responsibility. The latter is especially true if it's due to a coworker leaving, in which case the company will have extra incentive to retain you. It's also best to time the conversation when your boss is in a good mood or you're otherwise connecting well, ensuring that your boss will work to keep you happy.

Based on your relationship with your boss, this conversation can be in a scheduled 1-on-1, a walk-in to their office, or an ad-hoc meeting you put on their calendar. Start the conversation by saying you really enjoy working there and find the work rewarding, but you need to ensure it makes sense for you financially, so you are looking to increase your compensation. Then, delve into the points you've prepared on the value you add to the company and other salaries for comparison to the market.

You've done your research, so enter with confidence and keep the conversation short. Don't feel the need to talk to fill silences; you want to maintain the position of strength you've established with your talking points. The ideal outcome of this discussion is for your boss to let you know how much they value you as an employee and that they'll see what they can do about your compensation. After this, they will likely talk with their boss and HR, hopefully returning in a few days with a raise offer.

When asking for a raise, the best leverage you can have is other employment that you are legitimately considering. However, mentioning this to your boss is the equivalent of a negotiation sledgehammer. I don't recommend bringing up your other opportunities unless you are fully prepared to take them, as your current employer might be put off by your boldness.

In addition to seeking out raises, you can also ask for promotions or apply for other positions within your company. Financially, promotions are simply raises with a higher magnitude. They can really accelerate your net worth gain, and they're the fastest way to increase your income without switching companies.

Asking for a promotion isn't inherently different than asking for a raise; it just has a bit more magnitude. Since there are many different types of internal promotions, it's best to stay flexible and leverage whichever opportunity is first available to you. Your career advancement network, mentioned in the previous section, can help you identify these opportunities throughout your company. Some examples include:

- **Ascending to a higher level within your current role**: in many large companies, there are hierarchies of job levels or job classes that come with automatic salary increases. For example, accountants can often get promoted from a staff accountant to a senior accountant. Large financial companies often have Financial Analyst positions numbered 1-4, with Financial Analyst 4 being the most senior and highest paid. If your company has levels like this, it is the easiest promotion to ask for because you won't be required to do anything inherently different from what you're already doing, and your boss will be expected to promote a certain number of people each year.
- **Moving into management in your existing area**: if you are currently an individual contributor, one obvious promotion opportunity is to move into management. This is what people often think of when they discuss promotions, and the most direct ascension in your company would have you taking your boss's job. However, you shouldn't wait around for your boss to retire (or kick the can). They might be in that

same position for another 20 years. Rather, you should look diagonally, at other management openings in your area, to ensure your boss is not a roadblock. If you want to go this route, it will be important to demonstrate your leadership skills by taking the lead on projects and helping develop people.
- **Landing a higher position in a new function or department**: finally, you can shift to a new area within your company to get a salary increase. For example, I've worked with many product managers who started off as engineers or designers before moving diagonally into product management. A career shift like this will have implications for the jobs you can get in the future, so you should think through where it could take you in a few years. However, if you'll be making more money now and think it's a path you might enjoy, go for it.

When going for a management role or a new internal position, treat it more like an interview than you would a conversation asking for a raise. We'll get into the details of interview prep in the next chapter, but you should be able to clearly outline why you will succeed in the new role. Again, people will want to help you accomplish your goals, so if you let your career advancement network know you're aiming to move up in the company, they will help you find and land these opportunities. Also, don't be afraid to be blunt if an opportunity presents itself. For example, if your company opens a job posting for a new manager position, tell your boss and your boss's boss that you'd like to compete for the role. This is how my wife Rachel ascended into her first management position.

Let's look at another coworker of paralegals Juan and Mary, Amber, who started in the same position but actively sought out promotions. Like Mary, Amber earned 4% annual raises, but in her fourth year with the company, she became a senior paralegal, and in her eighth year became a paralegal manager. Here is a snapshot of her financial situation, with a comparison to Mary and Juan.

Amber: 4% Annual Raise, Promoted Year 4 and 8				
Year	Amber Salary	Amber Net Worth	Mary Net Worth	Juan Net Worth
1	$45,000	$6,000	$6,000	$6,000
5	$59,730	$55,498	$43,996	$35,817
10	$85,249	$219,128	$135,394	$89,779
15	$103,718	$528,546	$301,808	$169,580
20	$126,189	$1,035,019	$584,031	$286,048

By earning two promotions during her career, Amber attained a salary of $126,000, more than double Juan's and over $30,000 more than Mary's. Her net worth over that period also ballooned to over $1 million, about $450,000 greater than Mary's and **$750,000 greater than Juan's**.

As these examples show, earning raises and promotions is the fastest way to accumulate wealth within the same company.

Make the most of it

Everything so far in this chapter has been focused on increasing income at your current job. There are two additional actions you can take to make the most of your current situation:

- Make yourself more marketable for future jobs
- Leverage your non-monetary benefits to increase your effective income and saving rate

Make yourself more marketable for future jobs

To increase your market value, you should take advantage of your employer's education programs and other opportunities to increase your skillset. I mentioned previously that it often makes sense to pursue education that will automatically increase your pay. However, these opportunities are often beneficial even if they don't immediately result in a direct pay increase.

Many employers will pay for education that will help you do your job better, whether that means individual courses, industry certifications, or full-on degrees. If you have this opportunity, take it. When deciding what education to pursue, you should focus on what will increase your ability to land desirable, higher-paying jobs in the future. An easy way to determine this is to look at postings for jobs you would want and see what credentials they ask for.

Also, check if your company will pay at least a portion of a master's degree. This is a huge potential benefit that will greatly increase your career earning potential. Like any advanced education, master's programs can give you knowledge that can help you excel in your job. But even more importantly, they often tick a box for high-income positions and sometimes result in automatic salary increases. If you're worried about the time commitment on top of your already busy schedule, know that it's possible to find online or evening programs that will work for you. I completed my MBA online while working a full-time day job and spending over 20 hours a week on my sports betting side hustle. I did this without detracting from my other money-making endeavors by taking one class at a time over four years.

Even if your employer doesn't currently have formal education programs, they will likely support your desire to expand your skillset if you frame the request as meeting a business need. For example, you could approach your boss and say, "As refining processes is becoming a bigger part of my role, I think it's important I become an expert in process efficiency. Since we don't have any lean process experts internally, I'd like to attend Lean Six Sigma training to pick up best practices and help implement them throughout the company."

Taking this approach provides you with two major benefits. The first is that your boss and others will see you as a unique expert in a specific area (in this case lean processes), increasing your odds of receiving raises and promotions. The second is that you get to spend your workday improving your skills in a marketable area, meaning you'll be getting paid to increase your market value and your future income. That's pretty awesome.

Besides education opportunities, you can also make the most of your current job by working on high visibility projects. These types of projects translate very well to a resume, increasing your chances of landing higher-paying jobs in the future. Examples include launching a new product, expanding to a new market, or completing an acquisition. Any tech company would be interested in hiring someone who worked on the initial launch of the iPhone.

The final way you can increase your market rate at your current job is by making yourself well-known and recognized in your industry. This doesn't mean you have to become a celebrity like Elon Musk, but it is helpful to appear in industry blogs when someone Googles your name. An easy way to do this is to do a quick search for conferences in your industry and send the organizer an email volunteering to speak at the conference. This will likely get you a snippet on their website outlining how impressive you are and why people should listen to your session.

While you're at these conferences, take the chance to network with other companies and learn what they're doing. This can help in your current job, but more importantly, you can build relationships and gain connections that you can leverage to switch companies in the future. If speaking in front of crowds isn't your thing, you can look to write blog posts for your company website or industry publications. You don't have to be in marketing to do this; you can simply be a quoted subject expert.

Leverage your non-monetary benefits

In addition to increasing your market value, you can make the most of your current job by leveraging your benefits to increase your effective income. The most important benefit to take advantage of is your retirement savings plan, which can make a massive difference in your overall compensation package. I'll cover this in detail in Chapter 6, but the basic idea is to ensure you maximize any company match (free money!) and leverage your retirement accounts, like a 401k, to lower your taxes.

Beyond retirement saving, there are a few other common benefits to look for.

- **Pre-tax commuter and childcare benefits**: most companies offer the ability to pay for parking, mass transit passes, and daycare pre-tax. This reduces your taxable income by the amount of your expenses, saving you close to 40% depending on your marginal tax rate.
- **Virtual work**: another way to save on commuting expenses but also save time. If you can work from home one day per week or even full-time, that saves time commuting, getting ready for work, and helps you avoid low-value meetings and chatter. Historically, working virtually has hindered your chances to move into management, but that has changed during and likely after the 2020 coronavirus pandemic. Virtual work can be a particularly great advantage for those looking to spend more time on their side hustles.
- **Insurance**: many employers pay a large portion of employees' health insurance premium, so look for a plan that doesn't require you to pay much in premiums. I'll cover insurance in greater detail in Chapter 5.
- **Subsidized gym memberships or other health-related benefits**: many companies offer discounts or reimbursement for gym memberships, which could potentially save you close to $1,000 over the course of a year. Some companies also give discounts on health insurance premiums or provide Fitbits to employees who take certain health steps, like getting an annual physical or following an exercise program. Employers want a healthy workforce, so take advantage to stay healthy and save some money.

- **Other company discounts**: you might have access to negotiated deals with other businesses, particularly if you work at a large company. This can be particularly helpful for travel, such as hotels and rental cars. For example, I save a ton on car rentals from a corporate discount, sometimes getting a free upgrade to higher-end cars.
- **Employee Stock Purchase Plans (ESPPs):** some companies offer a plan that allows employees to purchase company stock at a discounted price. Because you can immediately sell the purchased stock at the higher market price, this is essentially free money on top of your salary.

In summary, you can make the most of your current job by developing marketable skills and leveraging your company benefits.

How I did it

I used the methods in this chapter to increase my compensation by 45% within two years at the same company.

I began my post-college life as a statistician at an insurance company, earning $55,000 a year. Immediately after starting, I looked for ways to increase my salary and learned that passing insurance exams resulted in automatic pay increases. That's all I needed to hear to buy a few textbooks and start studying, earning an extra $7,000 in my first year. I also learned about the company patent program, which paid out for invention ideas when a patent was submitted and again when it was approved. I couldn't understand why only a few employees were taking advantage of this, so I did some research on new technology impacting the insurance industry and submitted dozens of ideas resulting in over 20 patents. This made me an extra $25,000 over 2 years.

Not only did passing exams and submitting patents earn me money directly; they helped company leadership notice me, which led to earning high individual performance ratings. This ensured I maximized my annual bonus payout each year.

In addition to doing what I could on my own, I recruited others to help my career take off. As I shared earlier, I told my boss from the beginning that I wanted to make a big impact on the company and was striving to be in the C-suite someday. With that drive, a solid academic background, and some luck, I was chosen to participate in an executive prep program for select new hires. This allowed me to learn about different areas of the company and network with some bigwigs.

While that part sounds great on paper, I honestly hated networking. I would rather study for an insurance exam than talk to a Vice President about what motivates me. But I sucked it up and did the work to establish a solid network. To force myself to take action, I developed a list of the key people I wanted to keep in touch with, how often I was going to connect with them, and what I hoped to gain from the connection. This motivated me to overcome my natural introversion, schedule the meetings, and develop a leadership network, which paid off.

After about a year working full-time, I approached my boss about being promoted from a Statistician I to Statistician II based on the additional responsibilities I had taken on. Much to my surprise, I got the promotion without any qualms. That, combined with the exam increases and patent bonuses, brought my compensation to $68,000. That was great, but I knew I had to move into management if I really wanted to accelerate my career. Unfortunately, these promotions were slow-moving in my department. The typical manager had about the same tenure as Queen Elizabeth. So, I started looking to adjacent areas for openings, and underwriting seemed to be a good fit.

Being the independent 23-year-old that I was, I didn't ask for any help when first applying for an underwriting manager position using the internal company application system, which was basically the same as submitting a resume. I anxiously awaited a response for 3 weeks before I got an email saying they were moving forward with other candidates (likely with more than 2 years' experience).

At this point, I swallowed my pride and realized that I wouldn't be successful applying cold. I reached out to one of my VP connections from the executive prep program, who gave me some tips to improve my chances the next time. A couple months later when I let him know of a new opening I was gunning for, he called the hiring manager to provide a personal recommendation. Not only did I get an interview this time; I landed the job. This diagonal move within the company made me a manager, increased my pay to $80,000, and set me up for even higher-earning roles.

Since I had maxed out on my insurance exam increases, I sought out the next opportunity to increase my market rate. Recognizing that all the execs had a master's degree and most had finance backgrounds, I decided to get an MBA. As mentioned earlier, I was concerned about the time commitment and sought to complete the degree as efficiently as possible. I aggressively split up group work, only read the lecture notes, and generally did just what was needed to get a B, the minimum for my tuition reimbursement. This made school manageable on top of my day job and various side hustles.

After starting my MBA, I had a diversity of job experience, a broad understanding of the business, a solid leadership network, and would soon tick all the education boxes. Once again, I started asking around about how to get to the next level and make a bigger company impact. This led to me applying and getting an offer to start a new insurance company in San Francisco, which is where my income really took off.

While I was busy squeezing every dollar out of my job, Rachel was also making some great moves to set her up for success. She started her career as an accounting analyst and leveraged her company's education program to its fullest. She obtained her master's in accounting and then her CPA, which her employer paid for in full. During this time, she also made a lateral move from an analyst to a supervisor position. While that did not increase her salary at the time, it gave her leadership experience that increased her market rate. Armed with that experience and her new credentials,

Rachel landed a higher-level and higher-salary accounting manager position at a new company less than a year later. And this was all before I started sharing with her (or as she would say, forcing upon her) my goal of becoming a young millionaire.

In summary, I followed the advice in this chapter by doing what I was paid to do, showing my ambition, asking for raises/promotions, and making the most of opportunities to increase my marketable skills. Following these tips will help you optimize your day job and substantially increase your income. With just this first step complete, you'll already be on track to quickly become a millionaire. Next, we'll cover how you can further accelerate that timeline by switching jobs.

CHAPTER 2

Strategically switch companies for higher pay

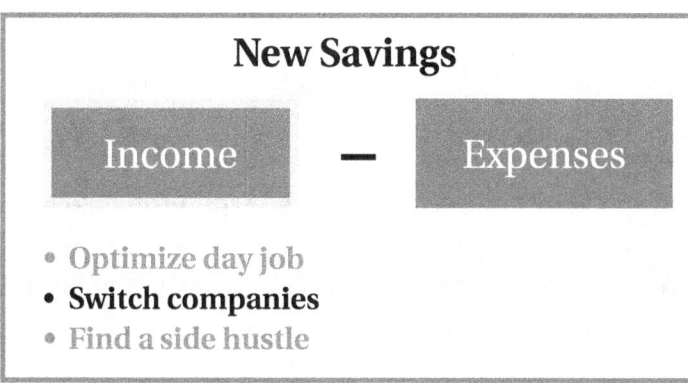

If I offered you a job paying $11,000 an hour, would you take it? Not many opportunities like this exist, but there is one available to you right now: putting in the work to find a new job. Odds are, you're currently passing up this $11,000 an hour opportunity. So, let's see where you're spending your work time instead.

I want you to do this calculation on your own, but I'll use some typical numbers as an example. Let's say you are normally at the office Monday through Friday, 8:00 to 5:00. That's 45 hours per week. When doing this calculation, most people stop there – failing to realize that the total time impact on your life is much greater.

If your commute is 45 minutes door-to-door, that's another 7.5 hours each week. And since your job is stressful and mentally exhausting, you need another 45 minutes to unwind before you can do anything useful at home. You then have the occasional last-minute request or phone call during your nights and weekends, adding another 4 hours per week. Adding this all up, you spend 64 hours of your week just to do your job. That is 3,200 hours per year.

Now let's calculate how much time you spend not necessarily doing your job, but instead optimizing your job situation. Again, you should do this calculation on your own, but in a typical example, let's say you spend 1 hour per month perusing job websites for any interesting opportunities. About once every 2 years, you decide it might be time to consider a new job, so you update your resume and LinkedIn, which takes 4 hours. Then you go through the interview process with 2 or 3 companies, taking you a total of 12 hours. That brings you to an average of 20 hours per year spent optimizing your job situation.

If this typical example is you, you are spending 3,200 hours doing your job and 20 hours optimizing your career every year. That means you spend less than 1% of your working time helping yourself and the other 99% helping your employer.

Remember that optimizing your income means managing your career like a business. The service you are selling is your employment. The time you spend improving your job situation is really time marketing your service. Most industries spend about 10% of their resources on marketing, and rapidly growing companies spend closer to 40%. By spending less than 1% of your time marketing your service, you're likely not managing your business effectively and are doing your career and your finances a disservice. Because this is true of most people in the workforce, that makes it easy to stand out and frequently switch jobs for higher pay, which is the number one way to increase your income.

Ultimately, there is only so much you can do to increase your salary at your current company in a short amount of time. You can get all the education possible, excel at your job, successfully ask for raises, and still end up with a salary only 6% higher than where you started. This is largely due to a concept known as "anchoring."

The basic premise of anchoring is that people rely too heavily on the initial information they had (the anchor) when making future decisions. It is impossible for them to get away from that anchor point. A study conducted by researchers Amos Tversky and Daniel Kahneman perfectly illustrates this bias. In the study, participants observed a spinning roulette wheel that randomly landed on either 10 or 65. After this, they were asked to guess the percentage of the United Nations that were African nations, a question completely unrelated to the result of the roulette wheel. Participants whose wheel stopped on 10 guessed 25% on average, while participants whose wheel stopped on 65 guessed 45% on average. These participants clearly knew the outcome of the roulette wheel had no bearing on the question being asked, yet their answers were heavily influenced by the number they saw; those who saw a higher number on the roulette wheel guessed a higher percentage. They were anchored to that higher point and couldn't move away from it.

Anchoring applies to your compensation, too, and the effect is even stronger than in the study. Rather than being completely random like the roulette wheel, there is some logic behind anchoring salaries. Your boss thinks "we were only paying him $50,000 last year, so there's no way he's worth $60,000 this year. The most we can do is a 6% increase."

The great thing about a new job is that it doesn't have that anchor point. Your potential employers don't know what you were paid two years ago; they just know a general market value for the skillset that you convince them you have. This is why the fastest way to increase your pay is to regularly change jobs.

According to Forbes, the average annual raise is 3%. With average annual inflation just over 2%, that means the real wage increase most employees see is 1% per year, which is disappointingly low. However, the average pay increase when switching companies is between 10% and 20%. That is a huge difference that compounds over the course of a career.

To illustrate that impact, let's revisit an example from last chapter. Recall that Juan is a paralegal at a large law firm and a company's dream employee: he performs his job well and doesn't ask for raises or look at jobs at other companies. He just takes his 2% raise every year.

Steven, on the other hand, very actively manages his career. He started as a paralegal at the same firm as Juan but accepted a senior paralegal job at a competing firm in his second year. While there, he took advantage of their education reimbursement program and earned a project management certification. This allowed him to switch companies once again for a pay increase in year 4, this time becoming a project manager at a large corporation. He went on to become a mid-level manager there and switched companies one more time during his career. Clearly Steven put more effort into his career than Juan, and their financial summary shows how well it paid off.

Year	Steven Salary	Steven Net Worth	Juan Salary	Juan Net Worth
1	$45,000	$6,000	$45,000	$6,000
5	$73,008	$90,964	$48,709	$35,817
10	$112,387	$366,512	$53,779	$89,779
15	$151,198	$910,893	$59,377	$169,580
20	$198,106	$1,876,032	$65,557	$286,048

Both Steven and Juan did a great job of saving based on their starting income of $45,000. But the extra saving and investing from Steven's job changes result in his net worth exceeding $1.8 million in 20 years. By intentionally switching companies for higher pay, Steven gained an extra $1.6 million in net worth.

The reason this worked out so well for Steven is that moving to a new company gives you a chance to sell yourself as an expert in something you've been able to master quickly. Steven's first firm knew he was sharp and that he was picking up project management skills, but they also knew he had only been doing it for 6 months. However, the companies where he applied for project management jobs just knew he had his certification and had successfully managed important projects, as his resume and interview illustrated.

In a fair world, it wouldn't matter how long you have been doing something – just how well you can do it. Actively searching in the job market gets as close as possible to this fantasy fair world. It also allows you to see how different companies get different value for the same skillset. For example, if you have a knack for digital marketing, that might be worth $50,000 to your local sporting goods store, but it might be worth $500,000 to Amazon. Only by searching and applying for new jobs will you be able to find the top end of your market value.

A common rebuttal to frequently changing jobs is that it will hurt your long-term career prospects because "no one wants to hire a job hopper." That may have been true in the 1960's when it was common to work for one company for 40 years and live off a pension in retirement, but it's not true anymore. In 2020, the average employee tenure is about 4 years, including later-career workers who tend to stay at one place longer. For those under age 40, the average tenure is closer to 3 years.

Statistics support frequent job changes, and my personal experience as a hiring manager reflects that, too. I've hired dozens of employees in my career, and I would take someone with 6 years' experience at 3 companies over someone with 6 years at 1 company every time. The "job hopper" will have a better view into industry best practices; it's more likely that he's taken the positives from each company and pieced them together to form his own working style. He's also proven the ability to integrate well in different teams and shown initiative as a "go-getter." The last thing I want as a manager is an employee whose goal is to just not get fired and coast to retirement in 20 years.

Clearly, switching companies can significantly improve your ability to accumulate wealth. So enough with the why; let's get to the how.

Do the prep work

The goal when preparing to apply for new jobs is to convince potential employers that you're worth the top of the market rate for your skillset. Most of the work to do that (resumes, interviews, etc.) revolves around selling the skills you have and takes only a few hours. However, you will need to dedicate some more time if you want to not only better sell your skills but also increase your market value.

In the last chapter, we discussed how to take advantage of opportunities from your current employer to make yourself more marketable, including getting more education and making yourself known within your industry. Each of these opportunities you take will increase your market value, meaning potential employers will pay you more. You should look for these even if your current employer doesn't pay for them, but you'll want to be more price-sensitive when paying on your own dime.

To determine what may be worthwhile, look at postings for jobs that you would like to have in a year or two and note the preferred qualifications. For example, if many jobs want some background in data science, you can complete a Coursera online learning program to become more proficient. If they want experience in a programming language you haven't used before, set out to learn it and apply it in a side project you can discuss during interviews.

The skills you pick up on your own and apply in creative ways will help you stand out in the job search. For example, I once interviewed a candidate who ran a gourmet s'mores catering company in addition to his typical product manager job. I gave him an offer and still remember him years later (and not just because I wanted him to bring s'mores into the office). His side gig showed his entrepreneurial spirit and ability to do a bit of everything, both important traits of a product manager. We'll discuss how to find a useful side gig in the next chapter.

Increasing your capabilities and expertise will certainly increase your market value, but it takes a long time. That's why the rest of the chapter is focused on the easier half of the equation: better marketing the value you already offer.

Just as you built your team of supporters at your current company, you'll also want to build a network of people who can help you land your next job. This is important so you can be referred for the job rather than being one of hundreds of cold applicants. Getting a referral from someone currently at the company significantly increases your odds of getting an interview and ultimately a job offer. According to a study from the Federal Reserve and MIT, referrals make up only 6% of applications but over 25% of new hires. That means getting a referral makes you *four times* as likely to land the job!

As mentioned before, I consider myself an introvert and hate most aspects of networking, especially forced small talk. If you're like me, you can still benefit from referrals with minimal pain by identifying a few key people who could help you with future employment and focusing on those relationships. These key people will generally be more senior than you and be able to influence the hiring process. A common example is a former boss or coworker who has moved on to a new company, ideally in a higher role. They could then hire you into that new company or at least provide a recommendation. One way to stay in touch with these folks is grabbing lunch a couple times a year to catch up and discuss your career progression. Often that conversation will spark a new opportunity for you.

If you happen to enjoy networking, feel free to ham it up and gain a few dozen connections; odds are, one of them will be helpful the next time you're looking for a job. If you're not a fan of these kinds of interactions, you can put the process of networking outside these key relationships on autopilot. When you meet new people through work, just add them on LinkedIn and reach out if you think they might be able to help you (for example, if a new role you want opens at their company). A quick way to build these potential connections is to attend industry conferences and add everyone you meet on LinkedIn.

Even if you don't know these connections well, they'll likely be happy to help as long as you were friendly when you met them. If you're hired, they may get a recruitment bonus, it makes them look good to their employers, and it just feels good to help people out. When you see you have a connection at a company you'd like to apply to, simply reach out and say you'd like to discuss the company and the role with them. After a short conversation, you'll likely have a referral. I landed my last job after getting a referral from my sister-in-law's former coworker, proving that it does not need to be a close connection to work.

After networking, the next step to prepare for a job change is to put real effort into demonstrating your value via your resume, cover letter, and interviews. These constitute the marketing material of your career.

In most cases, potential employers get their first impression of you from your resume, so that's where we'll start. I will go through what I consider important yet often neglected topics in resume optimization, but I won't cover the intricate details of formatting and organization. If you need some assistance on those aspects, a couple great resources are the Resumes Subreddit and The Muse.

The greatest opportunity to differentiate your resume from the rest of the pile is to customize it to the specific job you're applying for. Most candidates have a single, uniform resume that they use for all job applications. Using this method, they can hit *most* of the requirements of most jobs – but will likely not achieve 100% for any job. That is bad news for them and good news for you.

The resume that most candidates use to apply to jobs is what I consider my "base resume." This lists my most impressive accomplishments and highlights experience that is generally relevant to the type of position I'm applying for. For example, I had two base resumes for my most recent job search. One of these was focused on tech product management and highlighted how I delivered digital product features that improved the customer experience and increased customer retention. The other was focused on insurance positions and highlighted how I led a team of underwriters and actuaries to help build a startup insurance company.

Once you have your base resume complete, you can tweak it to focus on the specific requirements of the job you're applying for and include relevant keywords to ensure you get through automated filtering tools. For example, if the job posting says you'll be responsible for building a team in a new function, ensure you focus on your experience hiring and training new employees. If another position is an individual contributor role, focus more on your technical acumen. If you'll be responsible for running Google Ads campaigns, highlight the most successful campaign you've run. Once you nail these specific examples for a few jobs, you can start to reuse your arsenal of resume bullets to reduce this process to 5-10 minutes per new job application.

When writing these bullets, I recommend following the STAR method. STAR stands for Situation/Task, Action, Result.

- Situation/Task: what was the issue or challenge you were facing?
- Action: what did you do? (you specifically, not your team or your company)
- Result: what was the impact your action made? It's ideal to support this impact with numbers for as many bullets as possible.

Here are a couple examples from resumes I've used in the past.

- Led rollout of new auto insurance pricing initiative to over

- 2,000 agents and employees, improving retention and profitability of renewal business
- Built machine learning-based technical analysis system to beat college basketball spread markets, generating 400% ROI

You can see these were written to sound impressive. Your resume should be a collection of your most impressive accomplishments, not a mundane summary of your day-to-day work. For example, if you're a finance analyst, there is no need to waste a bullet with "Analyzed various sources of data to provide business insight to stakeholders." It's obvious you did that; that's what a finance analyst does. Instead, focus on specific projects or aspects of your job that are relevant. "Analyzed past financial statements and projected combined financials to enable acquisition of beverage brand, increasing company revenue by 23%." Using these techniques, you can make your resume as impressive as possible and ensure you clearly hit every qualification the company is seeking.

After updating your resume, you should next focus on your LinkedIn profile, which is essentially your online resume. If you don't yet have a LinkedIn profile, you need to create one. It doesn't matter if you don't like social networks. I don't either (I've been waiting five years for the right moment to post my first photo on Instagram).

LinkedIn is different than other social networks. Over 90% of recruiters actively use LinkedIn to source new hires. Even for the remaining 10%, having a complete LinkedIn profile is important for when someone Googles you, especially if you have a unique name. Your LinkedIn profile will likely be the first search result, ensuring that the company's first impression of you is a professional one. Admittedly, I have completely failed at this goal, since my first Google image result is a picture of me shirtless from my protein beer Kickstarter campaign. But apparently my LinkedIn profile was good enough to overcome that!

You don't need to spend much time on LinkedIn for it to be effective. Outside of adding new connections as previously mentioned, you can simply copy and paste the bullets from your resume. If you have multiple base versions of your resume like I do, you'll have to blend them together to ensure you have your most impressive bullets across each base resume represented.

The final step to optimize your LinkedIn profile is to go to your preferences and turn on the "open to new opportunities" option. This lets recruiters know that you're seeking employment and makes them more likely to reach out to you with opportunities. If you're worried about your current employer finding out you're searching, don't be. First, LinkedIn ensures you don't appear in searches from your current employer. Second, and more importantly, it's actually a *good* thing if your employer thinks you are looking. It forces them to assess your value to the company and gives you leverage to negotiate a raise or promotion.

With your resume and LinkedIn updated, the last piece of marketing collateral to create is a cover letter for jobs that ask for one. I know writing a cover letter is a pain, but you should always take the opportunity to upload a cover letter if you get one. You can keep it to 2-3 short paragraphs that highlight a couple of your most impressive and relevant accomplishments that can't fit into bullets on your resume. To save time and increase the number of jobs you can apply for, you can approach this the same way as a resume: create a base version or two that you then tweak for the specific job.

Selling yourself via your resume and cover letter gets you an interview; selling yourself in an interview gets you a job. Assuming, like me, you are more interested in getting a new job than getting a bunch of interviews, it is critical to prepare as well as possible.

The method I recommend for interview prep is to create a document for each company you interview with – using Microsoft Word, Google docs, or whatever works best for you. Use this doc to create detailed notes on your opening introduction. This is what you lead the interview with, and it can come in the form of questions like "tell me why you want to work here" and "what makes you a good fit for this role?" This should be a concise, impressive-sounding summary of what you've done in the past that builds up to you being the perfect candidate for the role. It is a sales pitch, not an autobiography.

In addition, prepare 5-10 hip-pocket examples to answer common behavioral and situational questions. These examples should be very specific and once again follow the STAR (Situation/Task, Action, Result) format. The exact questions will vary based on your role, but here are some common themes.

- How you can influence others or work well with a team
- When you faced a difficult challenge/conflict and how you overcame it
- Your greatest success or biggest impact you made on the company
- A time you failed and how you learned from it
- Recognizing inefficiencies and improving processes

Preparing for these generic examples is useful, but preparing for specific questions is even better. How would you like to know the questions on the test before you take it? If you're interviewing at medium-to-large companies, sometimes you can. Glassdoor has an interviews section where previous candidates recount their experience. Sometimes you'll get identical questions, but if not, you'll at least get a feel for the types of questions to prepare for.

The final step in preparing your interview doc is to add some company research and questions *you* can ask during the interview. Many hiring managers assess candidates by the pertinence of questions they ask, so incorporating your research will help you stand out against a candidate who asks how big the team is and how many vacation days they'll have. Here are a couple examples of simple questions incorporating a bit of research.

- What do you see as your biggest differentiators vs. (top competitor)?
- How has the launch of (new product) this year impacted the development roadmap? Do you expect to add new features to that or focus on new products?

It's helpful to know who you're interviewing with so you can prepare some questions specifically for them and prepare answers that better cater to their expertise. For example, if your first interview is with HR for a new accounting role, you probably shouldn't get into the details of how new SEC guidance changes how companies recognize foreign subsidiaries on their balance sheets unless you want your interviewer to fall asleep. But if you're interviewing with the technical accounting manager, that would likely have them on the edge of their seat.

As you progress into later rounds of interviews, you can use this doc to keep notes and reference earlier conversations. "From my conversation with Amanda, it sounds like one of the things you're really looking for is someone to own the overall product development process. I've set that up from scratch at my last two companies, and here is what I have seen work well…"

Like your resume, doing this interview prep becomes really easy after you interview a few times. You can copy 95% of your interview points from one job to the next, and explaining your situational examples will become second nature.

To understand the value of this prep work, let's revisit the calculation of how much time you spend each year improving your job situation. In my typical example, that was about 20 hours a year. Let's say after reading this chapter and understanding the importance of doing the work to switch jobs, you spend a total of 50 hours searching for jobs, fine-tuning your resume and interview skills, and interviewing at various companies. This is still a very small percentage of your overall work time. From doing all that work, you find a job with a pay increase of $15,000. That means your effective pay while optimizing your job situation is $300 per hour, only counting your extra money in the first year.

That is a pretty nice wage itself, but it doesn't tell the whole story. That $15,000 pay increase carries over and compounds for the rest of your career. An additional $15,000 in income might give you an extra $10,000 after-tax that you can save and invest. That invested money can then earn about 7% real investment returns per year. Also, over time, the $15,000 salary difference widens as you get percentage-based raises.

Over the course of 20 years, this compounding effect of both investment savings and annual raises nets you an additional **$550,000**. That means when you spent 50 hours to get that $15,000 salary increase, **you earned $11,000 per hour**!

When deciding how much effort you want to put into doing the prep work to switch jobs, ask yourself whether you want to do something that earns you $11,000 an hour.

Find the right job

Doing the prep work to land a new job also means taking the time to ensure it's the right job. Given this is a book about becoming a millionaire, I'm of course going to say salary is important. But it's not the only factor you should consider.

Recently when grabbing drinks with my friend Mike, I couldn't help but notice the bags under his eyes. It looked like he hadn't slept in days. He told me about his crazy travel schedule and 80-hour weeks that came with his management consulting job. He was exhausted but was slogging through it because it paid well. He was excited when a former coworker contacted him about a job that paid less than half as much but would be more relaxed, and he was considering taking it.

Obviously, Mike's current job was not sustainable for him, so he needed to make a change. But rather than telling him to take the new offer, I asked what other jobs he was considering. He said he wasn't actively looking, so this was the only job on the table.

Mike had created a false dichotomy of either continuing in the super stressful job or switching to a lower-stress job with half the pay.

When I pointed this out to him (in less direct terms), he seemed overwhelmed by the prospect of finding time in his busy schedule to search for jobs. But I suggested that he evaluate his priorities and make time for it, even if it means his performance at work might slip a bit. Mike took this to heart and started an earnest job search that week, and within a month and a half, he landed a new job at a former client that he really enjoyed. In that job, he's now making 10% more than he was as a consultant and working only 45-hour weeks.

Your job makes a massive impact on your finances and overall life satisfaction, so you shouldn't just take the first thing available because it's convenient. Spend the time to do an intentional job search and find the opportunity that is best for you.

When you're looking to make a move early in your career, you should apply to at least 25 (and preferably closer to 100) different jobs. This benefits you in three important ways.

1. It makes you more likely to get a job offer (which is the whole point of a job search)
2. It allows you to assess the top of your market value and get a feel for other non-salary perks companies are offering
3. Applying to many jobs within a short timespan maximizes the likelihood of getting two simultaneous offers, the ultimate situation for negotiating salary

Hopefully by now you're sold on doing a proper search and not just taking the first opportunity that pops up. With that established, let's discuss the mechanics of job searching.

The easiest way to search for jobs is to work with industry recruiters, who will do a lot of the work for you. I previously mentioned the power of referrals, and a recruiter recommendation is the next best thing. This will put your resume on the top of the virtual pile and is the fastest way to be exposed to many different opportunities without even spending time to apply.

Note that I am talking about external recruiters, not recruiters who work for a specific company. If you haven't worked with a recruiter before, the basic model is this: recruiters are contracted by employers to find them good potential employees and get them to apply to jobs. Recruiters are typically paid a percentage cut of your first year's salary, normally around 20%. So if you work with a recruiter who lands you a new job paying $100,000, the recruiter makes around $20,000. This means they will be more than happy to help you find a new job – it's literally their job to do so.

To find a recruiter, try Googling "recruiters for (industry/job) in (location)." Typically, that will pull up a few; if it doesn't, recruiters might not be prevalent for your industry. That is fine; you'll just have to do a bit more work on your own. If that search does pull up results, it's best to line up 1 or 2 recruiters and supplement with your own search (covered in detail below) to ensure you're exposed to many opportunities. After you've worked with a recruiter once, you can go back to the same one again when you're searching for your next opportunity. They'll be excited to work with you again since that means another paycheck coming their way.

In addition to working with a recruiter, you should do some searching on your own. Here are three sites that can serve as your job search foundation.

- **indeed.com**: Indeed is an aggregator of job postings pulled from company career sites, job boards, industry associations, and other sources. You can set up a job search on Indeed by title/keyword and location, then set up email notifications when a new job that matches is posted. Even when I'm not actively searching for a job, I keep a weekly digest from Indeed to stay aware of other opportunities.
- **Google jobs search**: another solid job aggregator. Just type "jobs" into a Google search bar and go from there. Google

partners with CareerBuilder, Monster, LinkedIn, Glassdoor, and a few others that make it a worthy complement to Indeed.
- **LinkedIn**: it's useful not only as your de facto online resume, but also to find jobs and apply to them very quickly. On their jobs section, you can perform a search and set up notifications, similar to Indeed. Also, as mentioned previously, be sure to mark yourself as open to new opportunities to help recruiters find you.

These three sites, plus a recruiter if you can find one, should be plenty to fill the front end of your job-searching funnel.

Before applying, it's worth doing some quick research up-front to help focus on the right opportunities. Most of the time, you should be able to find a salary range for your position on Glassdoor if it's not given in the job posting or job search website. If not, look at competitors and feel free to ask the recruiter at the company for the expected range to ensure you're in the same ballpark. It's worth finding out early if the company won't be able to meet your salary needs, since there is no point in moving forward with them. From there, your opportunities will get filtered down largely by which companies respond to you, but you also shouldn't be afraid to drop out of contention for a position you're no longer interested in.

After you find a job you're interested in, your next step should be to check your LinkedIn connections or even secondary connections (i.e. a connection of your connection) for anyone that works there. If you find a connection, simply reach out, say you're interested in X position, and ask if you can talk with them about the company. I have done this by reaching out to dozens of people I don't know personally, and I've only had one ignore me.

My final tip when working to find the right job and going through the application process: don't neglect the non-monetary aspects of the job. What do the Glassdoor reviews say about work-life balance? How does the location change your commute?

Answers to these questions can impact your life satisfaction, as well as your ability to earn more money outside your day job. Additionally, it's best to look for a job with strong advancement potential, ideally at a growing company or a growing function within an established company, which will help you ascend the career ladder faster.

Another non-financial aspect to consider is whether you think you will enjoy the job. This may seem obvious, but it's easy to get caught up in prestige and small monetary differences to end up in a job that's a terrible fit for you – as was the case with my friend Mike. Remember, money is a tool to get what you want in life, nothing more. If you find a job you genuinely enjoy, it's probably not worth switching to something you hate just so you can retire a couple years earlier.

Negotiate fiercely

By now, you've spent time perfecting your resume, doing interview prep work, and interviewing with a few companies. Finally, you've reached the end – you've received a new job offer! Getting to this point is a great accomplishment and a huge relief, but it's not time to let up just yet. It's time for final negotiations, where just a little extra effort can make a big impact on your compensation.

Here is a simple, 4-step process you can follow to maximize your compensation in a new offer.

1. Get a high initial offer by letting the company move first or setting a high anchor point
2. Line up competing offers from your current employer or other companies if possible
3. Leverage your competing offers or your current employment to ask for more compensation, without setting a number
4. Give a final amount that you would accept immediately

Let's look more closely at how each step works.

1. Get a high initial offer by letting the company move first or setting a high anchor point

At some point during the interview process, the company will ask what your salary expectations are. This may be a field you fill out on the application, or it may not be discussed until you're receiving an offer. The standard advice when negotiating is to let them give a number first so you can negotiate up from there. For example, when they ask what your salary expectations are, you could say something like "I expect to be compensated at the market rate for a (insert job) of my experience level." The logic behind this is that you don't want to throw out a number lower than what the company had in mind and set that as the anchor point.

However, that often doesn't work in practice, and the company will push you to give them a number. In that case, it's important to know two things: the company's general compensation range for this position and your market value (how much other companies would pay you). You should have an idea of the company range from your research up-front, either from Glassdoor, the job posting, or by asking HR to ensure you were in the same ballpark. You then want to shoot for the higher end of both your market value and the company range as a starting point. At this stage, only mention a number that you would be very happy to accept, since you'll likely end up a bit lower than the initial number you mention.

In this initial stage of negotiation, I recommend keeping the conversation focused on salary. You can save other aspects of compensation like bonuses to add into the mix later. For example, your initial response a question on salary expectation could be "based on my current compensation and experience working on (relevant aspect of your job), I'm looking for a base salary above $90k."

2. Line up competing offers from your current employer or other companies if possible

You never want to immediately accept an initial offer you receive. If you do, your new employer will likely be surprised and think they offered too high. Instead, say you're very excited about the opportunity to join and would like to take a few days to think through everything and talk it over with your spouse/family/cats/whatever. If the company has a problem with that (very few will), you likely don't want to work there anyway.

When negotiating anything, the best position to be in is to have legitimate alternative options you're considering. To do that, you can use the time between your offer and when you must respond to obtain a counteroffer from your current firm or a competing offer from another company.

To keep as many options open for as long as possible, it's best to seek a counteroffer from your current company without putting in official notice that you're leaving. You can do this by having a conversation with your boss that goes something like, "I really enjoy working here and want to stay with this team, but a recruiter recently reached out to me, and I ended up getting an offer that is much better for me financially. Is there anything the company can do so it would make sense for me financially to stay here?"

In addition to seeking a counteroffer from your current employer, you can use this time to speed up the process with any other companies you're talking to. Since the cat is out of the bag about you potentially leaving, you can aggressively schedule more interviews. To get other companies to speed up, tell them you're really excited about the possibility of working there but have another offer that you need to decide on by a certain date. That company will then do all they can to move up any interviews and get you an offer during that timeframe. And as an added bonus, they will likely see you as an even more desirable candidate now. Everyone wants what they can't have, even in business.

In an ideal world, you'll have a couple offers on the table plus your current employer to consider. That will give you maximum negotiating leverage and allow you to compare and select the role you'll most enjoy. However, timing makes it very difficult to get to that ideal world. Most companies will want to hear back within a week or so from when they give you an offer. If you're in this situation and are unable to speed up the process with another option you'd prefer, your best bet is to be up-front with the company who has given you an offer. Tell them you're excited about joining but want to see the process through with another company to ensure you're making the best decision. It may be a turn-off to them to be seen as a backup option, so I only recommend this if you strongly prefer another job you're interviewing for.

3. Leverage your competing offers or your current employment to ask for more compensation, without setting a number

Getting another offer at the same time is ideal but difficult. If you can't swing that, that's okay. You still have negotiating leverage. The company needs to entice you to accept their offer over staying at your current job or waiting for another company's offer. This leverage enables you to ask for more compensation over their initial offer, even if you would secretly be happy with that initial offer (don't tell them that). I mentioned earlier to focus on negotiating base salary first, and this is the time you pull in those other aspects as reasons to ask for more compensation. Here are some examples to consider bringing up:

- The value of the pension or 401k matching you're giving up (including how much more it would be worth if you stayed and accumulated more tenure)
- Your annual bonus which is due to be paid in two months
- Your additional commuting time and expenses
- Any other benefits, such as tuition reimbursement, paid time off, working from home, gym memberships, etc.

Regardless of the reasons you give when asking for more compensation, it's best not to give a set number that you're asking for when responding to an initial offer. Instead, simply say you will need more compensation to make the financials work for you. This puts the ball back in their court to return with a higher number and gives you one final card to play.

4. Give a final amount that you would accept immediately
At this point, the company has given you an initial offer and hopefully a second offer with slightly higher compensation (that may be in the form of higher salary or a one-time signing bonus). The company has put a lot of time and money into recruiting you to join the team, and the hiring manager is likely getting a bit anxious about whether you'll join. That's what makes it the perfect time for one last negotiation move – tell them an offer that you would accept immediately.

Assuming the prior offer was already a satisfactory jump from your current compensation, this final amount should only be a bit higher than your most recent offer. You're likely approaching the company's limits, which is exactly where you want to be. For example, you could say "I'm really excited to join and appreciate all you've done to make this work. I just need to ensure the financials make sense for me personally. If you could do $100k base salary with a $10k signing bonus, I'd happily accept the offer today." This will give the hiring company a choice to either meet your request and have a new employee locked in or to continue in the uncertain negotiation stages. Most will choose the former.

Following these negotiation techniques, it's common to get a 10%+ higher starting salary than what you were initially offered, often with other added bonuses. Here's an example of how I used this 4-step process to negotiate a higher salary moving from San Francisco to Chicago.

With a background in both tech product management and insurance, I applied for over 50 positions spanning a wide variety of companies. I leveraged a connection for a referral whenever possible. The first offer I received was from an insurance company, with an annual salary of $175,000 and a 20% annual bonus target. At that time, I was in the late interview stages with a sports data company (which sounded a lot more exciting than insurance), so I let them know I had another offer on the table and asked if we could accelerate the process to wrap up within the next week.

They were happy to do that, and at the end of the week I received an offer of $180,000 annual salary with a 20% bonus. Armed with that offer, I went back to the insurance company and let them know I had a higher offer on the table, asking for a base salary of $190,000. Within two days, I had a new offer from the insurance company for $185,000 base salary. I then told the sports data company that I had a financially better offer (without giving a precise number) and asked if they could go any higher. They shortly came back with $190,000 base salary.

This already matched what I was making in San Francisco, so I was ecstatic. However, I knew I could squeeze out a bit more with a final negotiation. I told the sports data company that if they could offer $190,000 base salary with a 30% bonus target (up from 20%) and a $10,000 signing bonus, I'd sign immediately. I had that exact offer in front of me before the day was over.

In total, I spent about two hours doing some salary research, preparing talking points, and speaking on the phone with recruiters at the two companies during this stage. Those two hours netted me an additional $47,000 in compensation, which is the easiest money I've ever made.

Consider new geographies and careers

In addition to switching companies, there are some bigger life and career changes you can consider to really ramp up your income.

The first of these is expanding your geography, which was key in my journey to $1 million. I mentioned earlier that your skillset is likely worth more to certain employers than it is to others. In the same vein, your skillset is likely worth more in certain locations. This is due to concentrations of companies that are all competing to hire employees with similar skills. For example, there is a dense concentration of software and technology companies in the San Francisco Bay Area, resulting in high software engineer salaries. Similarly, investment bankers and finance professionals can often maximize their income in New York.

When expanding your geography, you could cast a wide net and consider jobs across the country. However, that will likely prove overwhelming. Plus, do you really want to live in Bessemer, Alabama? I didn't think so.

Instead, I recommend choosing one or two additional markets outside your current home base that you would enjoy and have solid career prospects for you. For example, if you work in technology you might decide that the Bay Area or the growing tech hub of Austin, Texas, would be great places to live in addition to your current city of Indianapolis. You could then focus your job search in those three locations.

You might think I'm crazy for recommending someone move to these ultra-high-cost-of-living areas to save more money. It definitely goes against conventional wisdom. But in this case, conventional wisdom is wrong.

While it's true that the cost of living is higher in these locations, the financial impact of increased expenses is often exaggerated relative to the additional income you can earn. Many people think that if expenses are twice as high, your income must be twice as high to come out ahead. However, that's only true if you're spending every penny you earn. When you're saving some of your money, it's the absolute dollar difference that matters. To illustrate, let's look at Ted, who is considering moving from New Haven, Connecticut, to Manhattan for a higher-salary job.

Wolfram Alpha's cost of living calculator tells us that the cost of living in Manhattan is about double New Haven. The website also includes a nifty category breakdown if you'd like to customize the estimate based on your spending, but we'll go with the standard for now. If Ted is earning $50,000 in New Haven and is offered a job making $90,000 in Manhattan, should he take it?

To answer that question, we need to know Ted's expenses. In New Haven, Ted earns $50,000 and spends $35,000 a year, saving $15,000 annually. We can use the cost of living indexes to estimate annual saving after the move.

Ted Moving Calculator			
	New Haven	Manhattan	Brooklyn
After-Tax Salary	$50,000	$90,000	$90,000
Cost of Living Index	1.00	1.95	1.48
Expenses	$35,000	$68,250	$51,800
Saving	$15,000	$21,750	$38,200
Saving Rate Increase	0%	45%	155%

If he moved for the new job in Manhattan, Ted would earn $90,000 and spend $68,000 a year. That leaves him with $22,000 left to save, increasing his saving rate by 45%. And that's if Ted lives in Manhattan. If he instead lives in Brooklyn and makes the short commute to his Manhattan office, he would spend $52,000 and save $38,000 a year, increasing his saving rate by 155%!

With this saving rate – even if Ted earns no additional income beyond his day job and averages 6% annual raises – he should have a net worth over $810,000 in just 10 years, becoming a millionaire before year 12. If he had instead stayed in New Haven, he would have a net worth less than half that, $360,000. This example shows how increased income in these areas can easily outweigh the increased expense, especially for people who already save a portion of their income.

Of course, high-income locations are often large cities, and they might not be your cup of tea. Even so, it is worth considering working in a higher income area for a few years before moving to a more desirable, lower-cost area. In addition to helping you save more while living there, this strategy also sets a high anchor point for your salary. When moving to a lower-cost area, you may see a salary cut, but it will often be much smaller than you'd expect. You can use the anchoring bias in your favor.

When interviewing for jobs in the lower-cost area, you can say something like, "I understand salaries aren't as high here, but I'm currently at $x and am looking to come as close to that as possible." Using this method, combined with some fierce negotiation, I was able to get a small salary **increase** when I moved from San Francisco to Chicago.

One additional aspect to consider is whether you can find remote work and obtain a higher salary without necessarily increasing your cost of living. Remote work is becoming much more common after the 2020 coronavirus pandemic, but as of the writing of this book, most companies still pay virtual employees based on where they live. They do this for a couple of reasons. The first is that the company is competing for your employment with other companies in your area and must pay a competitive salary. The second is that the world has not yet fully adapted to virtual work.

Each situation is different, but you may be able to use this to your advantage. For example, a company based in Seattle that allows remote work may use the same salary ranges for all its employees in the state of Washington. If that's the case, working remotely in Spokane, which has a cost of living index 33% lower than Seattle, will be incredibly advantageous financially. Remote work standards are rapidly evolving, so it's worth considering this possibility and doing the math as outlined in Ted's example above to determine the job and location combo that works best for you.

In addition to considering new geographies to increase your income, you can also consider a new career path. While it's true that people in almost any industry can follow the advice in this book and become millionaires, there is no denying that it is faster and easier in some career paths than others. If you're currently a retail cashier, it is a very arduous climb to get your income high enough to develop substantial savings that can then earn investment returns. If you're currently earning a low income and don't see a clear path to increase it, a career change may be your best option.

When deciding if you should pursue this route, you'll want to check how the math works out, including the opportunity cost – that is, the income you will lose by withdrawing from the workforce to pursue the education or training you'll need. In general, it is best to minimize the time you're spending money rather than earning it, meaning full-time school is often not ideal. Even if you're only earning $40,000 a year, spending two years as a full-time student paying $25,000 a year in tuition means that you're effectively paying $130,000 for that education, considering the opportunity cost. That $130,000 could instead be invested in the market and making you more money.

While it's possible that additional full-time education will work out in the long run if your income increases enough, the economics work much better if you're able to do night/weekend classes without leaving the workforce. For example, if you're currently a cashier at a retail store, could you take some community college classes and move into an HR position at that store? If so, after a year or two you will be an experienced HR professional with relevant education. That opens up many more doors, such as advancing into higher store management or starting in a corporate HR position.

When analyzing these decisions to determine the best financial path, you will need to consider differences in income and expenses each year moving forward to calculate how much you will be able to save. You then compound your saved amount by your expected investment returns to calculate expected net worth over time. This is the same calculation that I have shown at the start of every section of this book. Whichever path gets you to your desired net worth faster is the financially superior route.

Here is an example of three teachers making different career decisions. Each of them starts off with a $50,000 pre-tax income and $30,000 of expenses. Outside of their career changes, they earn a 4% annual raise.

In this example, Joe is our base case. Unlike the others, he stayed in his position as a teacher throughout his career, so his salary increases were solely due to the 4% annual raises. He kept his expenses low, and with his gradually increasing income was able to approach $670,000 net worth in his 20th year working.

Joe: Did Not Switch Careers			
Year	Income	Education Expense	Net Worth
1	$50,000	-	$7,500
2	$52,000	-	$16,425
3	$54,080	-	$26,923
4	$56,243	-	$39,154
5	$58,493	-	$53,291
10	$71,166	-	$159,740
15	$86,584	-	$349,712
20	$105,342	-	$667,959

Caroline, on the other hand, decided to pursue an adjacent career in education administration. She got her master's degree in the evening, almost entirely reimbursed by the school she was teaching at, which gave her an automatic $10,000 salary increase. Two years after completing her master's, she applied for dozens of administrator jobs and became an assistant principal in a new district, nearly doubling her income in 5 years. Caroline's career shift paid off, as she reached $1.3 million net worth in 20 years.

Caroline: Masters Degree in Evening			
Year	Income	Education Expense	Net Worth
1	$50,000	$3,000	$4,500
2	$52,000	$3,000	$7,615
3	$63,000	-	$21,036
4	$65,520	-	$36,536
5	$88,000	-	$68,221
10	$107,065	-	$294,942
15	$130,261	-	$678,359
20	$158,483	-	$1,298,041

Tim wanted a change from his job as a political science teacher and thought, given his background, the next logical step was to become a lawyer. He applied and was accepted to a private law school and took out loans to cover the $65,000 annual tuition over the next 3 years. After graduating law school, he found a job making $85,000, a 70% increase from his salary as a teacher. However, his incurred costs and opportunity costs were significant setbacks. He spent nearly $200,000 to attend law school and during that time earned only $20,000 from a legal internship. Even with his higher income, he had a negative net worth at year 10 due to his student loans. At year 20, he was earning $160,000 a year but was still in a worse financial position than Joe, who had remained a teacher throughout his career.

Tim: Full-time Law School			
Year	Income	Education Expense	Net Worth
1	-	$65,000	-$95,000
2	-	$65,000	-$190,600
3	$20,000	$65,000	-$272,812
4	$85,000	-	-$245,148
5	$88,400	-	-$215,741
10	$107,552	-	-$39,543
15	$130,854	-	$215,050
20	$159,203	-	$650,896

This example shows why it is often financially unwise to return to school full-time. Even if you substantially increase your earning potential, the lost income and the cost of education, combined with the impact of compounding investment income, are tough to overcome.

In addition to calculating which option is financially superior, you should remember that there are more important things in life than finance. There is no doubt that switching geographies or career paths can significantly boost your net worth. However, you should only make these changes if you believe it will improve your overall life satisfaction, not just to make more money. As you start to accumulate wealth and are on the path to financial independence, you will feel increasingly free to make these decisions that may not benefit your wallet but instead benefit your life.

Practice makes perfect

You now know how you can effectively switch jobs to rapidly increase your income. But having a plan is only the start; you need to execute that plan.

Marketing yourself by crafting a solid resume, impressing companies during interviews, and successfully negotiating are all acquired skills. If you've never put much effort into these things before (which is true of most people), you likely won't be good at them starting out. But that is still infinitely better than those who don't give it a shot. As you go through this process a few times and interview with more companies, your skills will quickly improve.

To keep these skills sharp (and, more importantly, to maximize your income), I recommend actively searching for new jobs and interviewing at other companies **at least** once every 2 years – even if you like your current job. The best time to apply for a new job is when you don't need one. If you're in a solid position now, you can tell recruiters and prospective employers than you need a salary 30% higher than what you make currently (without telling them it's so much higher). Then you either stay in your current job you enjoy or make 30% more money, and either way you discover your fair market rate. It's a win-win.

I know it may seem like a daunting task to spend time job searching on top of your already stressful workweek. However, you ultimately need to prioritize what is important in your life, even if that means your performance at your current job falls off a bit during this time. This doesn't mean you should blow off work for a week to interview without any notice, but it does mean you might ramp your effort down to 80-90% for a couple months while you focus on applying for jobs and interviewing.

Remember, you should manage your career like you manage a business and make decisions that are best for your career. It would be irresponsible of you as a business owner if you didn't spend time marketing your services and ensuring you're being paid adequately. Ultimately, you must be proactive in managing your career, and now is the best time to start.

How I did it

Strategically switching jobs to increase my income was the number one reason I reached $1 million net worth at age 28.

Growing up constantly competing with two brothers, I always did whatever I could to win. This drive translated to my career, where I continuously look for ways to advance and improve my financial situation. It didn't take me long after entering the workforce to recognize the massive advantage gained by those who intentionally took the time to market themselves and increase their income, so I have put all my energy into doing just that.

As mentioned last chapter, I quickly moved around within my first company and gained broad experience across insurance, technology, and product management. I also took advantage of the education reimbursement program to earn my MBA and increase my market value. While both of those helped me increase my income within the company, I realized I could make a lot more money outside small-town Illinois and started searching for opportunities in more lucrative locations. This led to me applying for and ultimately accepting a job to help start a new insurance technology company in San Francisco.

This jump to a more senior job level and move across the country provided a major boost to my income. The new job had a base salary of $150,000, about double what I was making previously. It also included a generous relocation package to cover the move and help with the cost of living difference. Once I subtracted the expenses from my luxurious moving experience (that included both a U-Haul rental and Taco Bell stops along the way), I had a sizable lump-sum left over to invest.

Moving from central Illinois to San Francisco, my salary wasn't the only thing that increased. My monthly rent went from $400 to nearly 10 times that (albeit now split with Rachel). This is a perfect example of why I mentioned earlier that it's not the percentage increase in expenses that matters, but the absolute dollar difference. My last year in Illinois, I earned a total of $85,000 from my employer (about $60,000 after tax), and my expenses were $22,000, allowing me to save $38,000. My first year in San Francisco, my total compensation from work was $190,000 (about $130,000 after tax), boosted by my annual bonus and relocation payment. My expenses shot up from $22,000 to $54,000, but I still saved $76,000.

Even though my rent was 10 times higher and my total expenses doubled, I was able to save twice as much due to my higher-paying job. Not only did the move increase my net worth accumulation rate immediately, it also helped me set a high anchor point for my income, which paid dividends as I moved on to other jobs.

After completing a successful year at the new job, I decided it was time to ask for a raise. I now had experience in data science and technology leadership, giving me a high market value, especially in a tech hub. I had been contacted by industry recruiters and knew that a few competitors were paying higher salaries, albeit for more experienced positions. Regardless, I talked to my boss, outlining my contributions to our early success and the fact (or at least my opinion) that I could earn more elsewhere. I said that I wanted to stay but it didn't seem to make financial sense unless they could increase my pay. That conversation netted me a 15% salary increase without switching companies. That raise came at a perfect time: the same year Rachel and I got married. It was helpful covering the insane expenses of a wedding (one thing we did not do frugally).

While Rachel and I were doing great financially, we started thinking about the most important aspects of our lives, outside of money. We realized that we missed our family and friends back in our hometown of Chicago. So, we made it a priority to move there as soon as we could.

I updated my 3 base resumes covering statistics, insurance, and product management and started applying for jobs. I found the search more difficult this time, as I tried to find something that could come close to my San Francisco salary. I spent 4 months actively searching, including interviewing with 11 different companies. It was during this search that I realized how much my job searching and interviewing skills were improving with practice. I could hear myself speaking more confidently and more naturally working in my best examples with each interview. I also leveraged an industry recruiter during this search, though it was ultimately a referral from my sister-in-law's former coworker (whom I had never previously met) that landed me a job leading the product management team at a sports data company. After some negotiating, I ended up with a slight pay increase, which shows how you can use anchoring bias to your advantage.

Unfortunately, this move was one of my career misses. Despite being ecstatic about working in the sports industry, I struggled to deal with the long hours and high-stress environment, especially when compounded by some family health issues. This came to a head when, after working my usual 60-hour Monday-through-Friday week, I was planning to take a rare weekend off to visit my dad in the hospital. That Saturday morning, I received a series of frantic texts from my boss and the CEO about a presentation we needed to prepare and deliver in London the next week. After initially saying I couldn't do it, I caved to their pressure and cancelled my visit. Instead of visiting my dad in the hospital, my weekend was spent working on that analysis before flying to London Sunday night.

Reflecting on that decision during my flight back to the States, I knew I needed a change. Because I had been so diligent about saving, I was confident in my financial position and ability to move to a lower-stress job, even if it meant taking a pay decrease. I once again started my job search, subtly cutting back my time at the office to prepare and interview.

This time around, I wasn't looking to maximize my salary. I found an insurance technology company with much more relaxed leadership and an overall chill culture that seemed to be a great fit. To top it off, I was able to negotiate the same base salary I had previously (although with lower total cash and the upside of startup equity). I made this move just 9 months after starting the last job, which illustrates how the "job-hopper" stigma is largely a myth and can be easily explained away in an interview. It also once again showed how anchoring bias can be helpful. Achieving a high income initially can be hard, but *keeping* a high income is much easier.

At every new company I moved to, I used my 4-step system to negotiate a higher salary, each time landing an offer at least $10,000 higher than the initial offer. In the example I gave earlier this chapter, the final offer was a whopping $47,000 higher. Across 3 job changes, that amounted to an extra $75,000 in salary – simply from negotiating well.

Rachel also leveraged job-switching to her advantage, and she had the more difficult task after following my career moves across the country. I mentioned previously how she increased her market value by getting her master's and CPA paid for, landing an accounting manager job shortly after. She also leveraged her high San Francisco salary as an anchor point during our move to Chicago, taking only a slight pay decrease to go with the significant reduction in cost of living. A year-and-a-half after that move, Rachel started searching again, using an accounting industry recruiter. She ultimately accepted a job with a 30% higher base salary and amazing retirement saving benefits, which I'll discuss in detail in the investing section. When accounting for these benefits, her total compensation was 50% higher.

Both of our experiences show the power of proactively managing your career to ensure you're paid at the top of your market value. Doing this early sets a high anchor point and gives you optionality in your life progression.

By doing what's best for you, not for your employer, you can maximize your personal profit from your day job. That alone can make you a millionaire, but you can increase your income even further by finding a lucrative side hustle, which is our next topic.

CHAPTER 3

Find a lucrative side hustle

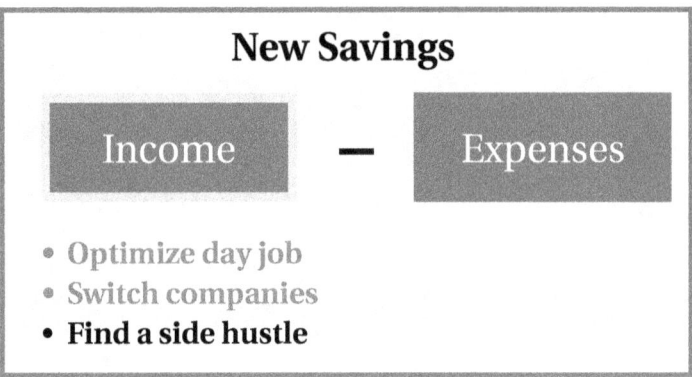

- Optimize day job
- Switch companies
- **Find a side hustle**

To optimize your income, you should manage your career like you would manage a business. I know I sound like a broken record, but it's worth repeating. This mindset is the driving force behind the three outlined methods to increase income, and it is especially important for the final method: earning money through a side hustle.

If you only sell the service of your employment to one buyer—your employer—you're not maximizing your personal profit. Great businesses diversify their income. Amazon, for example, earns income through membership subscriptions, online retail, book publishing, grocery sales, tech infrastructure, and more. They sell these many products to many different buyers. The customer buying *The Lion King* on Prime Video is not the same as the customer buying Amazon Web Services cloud computing infrastructure.

If you, as an employee, have multiple skillsets that you are looking to sell, it's unlikely you'll find the right buyer in a single employer. My friend Jason is a great example of this: he is a data scientist by day and a children's book author by night. He is passionate about both jobs, flexing his analytical skills in the office while channeling his imaginative side writing books. Unfortunately, there aren't many companies looking to hire someone to do a bit of data analysis and book writing. Since Jason can't package these services together to sell to one employer, he leverages a side hustle to make money doing both and maximize his personal profit.

By maximizing your profit and managing your career like a business, you're following an entrepreneurial mindset. Once you start making money outside your day job through a side hustle, you're not just following the mindset; you are a true entrepreneur. When people think of entrepreneurs, their minds often go to the ultra-famous and ultra-wealthy like Elon Musk or Bill Gates. While these are undoubtedly fantastic entrepreneurs, you don't need to build a billion-dollar empire to be successful. If you can find a way to generate any additional income outside your day job, that will make a massive difference in your ability to quickly accumulate wealth. This is because any income you earn from a side hustle is "extra" income. Assuming you're able to cover your expenses through your primary job, this extra income can go straight into your investment portfolio, which compounds over time to provide substantial wealth.

While it is certainly possible to become a millionaire without ever earning income outside your day job, having a side hustle greatly increases your chances and accelerates the process. In fact, people who earn additional income from some form of self-employment or business ownership are four times more likely to be millionaires than those who don't (research from Thomas Stanley and William Danko, authors of *The Millionaire Next Door*).

To illustrate the financial impact of a side hustle, let's look at an example. Shelly and Dave are both early-career registered nurses with a salary of $50,000 and annual expenses of $30,000. Dave is known as the "computer whiz" around the hospital and often helps troubleshoot IT issues for other nurses and the front desk staff. This isn't one of his official responsibilities, so he isn't paid any extra for it. However, since his nursing job is 4 days a week, Dave thought he could use his off day to make some extra money on the side. He found a niche market helping small businesses and individuals with large homes set up their internet networks and cabling. Working an average of 10 hours a week on this IT side gig, Dave earned an extra $10,000 a year. While he was earning a lower hourly rate than he did as a nurse, Dave enjoyed the work as a good change of pace from his nursing job.

Shelly, like most people, did not work a side hustle, earning all her income through her nursing job. Let's see how their finances evolved over time.

	Shelly	Dave
Primary Income	$50,000	$50,000
Side Hustle Income	-	$10,000
Annual Expenses	$35,000	$35,000
Annual Saving (after taxes)	$5,000	$13,000

Net Worth		
Year	Shelly	Dave
1	$5,000	$13,000
5	$38,935	$88,508
10	$125,500	$255,341
15	$288,236	$543,727
20	$569,466	$1,017,082

Both Shelly and Dave were successful financially due to their ability to maintain low expenses. However, Dave's side hustle propelled him to an impressive net worth of $1 million, nearly 80% greater than Shelly's. How is that possible when Dave earned just 20% more income?

While the extra $10,000 from Dave's side gig increased his income by 20%, the impact on his *saving rate* was much greater. Because all his extra after-tax earnings can go straight to his savings, his annual saving rose from $5,000 to $13,000, a whopping 160% increase. This metric of saving rate is more important than overall income. For each year Dave works, he can add $13,000 to his net worth (ignoring investments). Shelly, on the other hand, needs to work nearly three years to net the same $13,000. That is the magic of extra income from a side hustle – even a modest increase can dramatically raise your saving rate.

Accumulating wealth more quickly led to another significant benefit for Dave: he was able to retire from his nursing job after 20 years. He felt comfortable doing this because of the additional net worth he had accumulated as well as his desire to continue his IT side gig for 10 hours a week. This is often referred to as semi-retirement, which is a great way to free up time while still earning some income and increasing your net worth. As will be discussed in Chapter 9, this additional income, though small, makes a huge impact on your ability to retire because it reduces the amount that must be withdrawn from your investment portfolio each year. Shelly, on the other hand, needed to work another 5 years for her portfolio to surpass $1 million and grow large enough for her to comfortably retire. By finding a lucrative side hustle that he enjoyed, Dave essentially earned an extra five free years of his life.

Dave's IT business also provides a good example of one of the indirect benefits of side hustles: mental variety. Personally, I could easily work 40 hours per week in insurance and 20 hours in sports data modeling, but spending 60 hours doing either would be a real slog. It turns out this feeling isn't unique to me and is supported by scientific research.

Doing different types of activities that stimulate your brain can help you enter a state that scientists refer to as "the flow." When you're in the flow, you're entirely focused and immersed in an activity, often losing track of time. According to Harvard Medical School professor

Carol Kauffman, "The lost sense of time in flow state restores your mind and energy. It also requires a high level of concentration, and can enhance your creativity, help you think more clearly and sharpen your focus." Thus, finding a side hustle that you are really into is good for your mental health and your primary job performance.

Clearly, there are many benefits to having a side hustle, but the three we will focus on here are the ones that will help you on your mission to accumulate wealth.

1. A side hustle makes you more money today

This one is pretty obvious. Putting in more work as part of a side hustle earns you additional income. But as we discussed in the Shelly and Dave example, income from a side hustle is even more impactful than income from your day job when it comes to increasing your saving rate and wealth accumulation. Since you can cover your expenses with your primary income, 100% of your side earnings (after tax) can go straight into your investment portfolio. The example with Dave's IT side gig illustrated this well: by increasing his income 18% through a side gig, his saving rate went up 57%.

That extra money you save today then has time to compound as part of your investment portfolio. Each additional $10,000 after-tax you make through a side hustle, when compounded for 7% investment returns, results in an extra $400,000 over the course of 20 years.

2. A side hustle can drive success in your primary career

According to Warren Buffet, "the most important investment you can make is in yourself." Starting a side hustle is investing in yourself. Besides making you money directly, it can also help you earn more in your day job because of the additional skills and experience you gain. Running a business is like earning an MBA from the School of Hard Knocks. You are forced to learn the basics of entrepreneurship, including marketing, finance, and many other aspects of running a business. Naturally, these translate well into any job and are particularly helpful in advancing into high-paying corporate leadership positions.

In addition to gaining entrepreneurial skills, you can also leverage a side hustle to add to your technical skillset. For example, if you're a software engineer, you could use the skills gained through a side hustle as a designer to become an amazing front-end engineer with an eye for aesthetics. You can also enter a completely new field or industry, like I did with my move into the sports industry. I would not have been a very desirable candidate to a sports data company with a background solely in insurance. However, my side hustle of creating predictive models for sports betting made me a natural fit. The ability to work across multiple industries is helpful during a job search because you have many more potential employers, raising your market value.

3. A side hustle can help you find your passion

Starting a side hustle is the best way to find out if it's possible to make money doing what you *truly* love. Side hustles give you a low-risk way to test a new idea, without quitting your day job, to see if you really enjoy it and can earn a profit. Of course, you can do some research up front to ascertain that your passion for underwater basket weaving is unlikely to earn you substantial income. But if you're passionate about something, it doesn't hurt to give it a shot and see how much money you can make. For example, I have met people with very successful side gigs selling handmade crafts on Etsy and restoring antique cars.

Finding a lucrative side hustle can also help you pursue even those passions that don't make money after you've built up some savings. For example, a former late-career coworker of mine started an insurance industry blog on the side that took off in popularity and advertising revenue. With this newfound income, he was able to quit his day job and instead generate $30,000 per year working only 10-15 hours per week on his own schedule. This meant he had an extra 40+ hours of free time each week to pursue his passions like hiking and camping without having to worry about making money. He often brags to me about writing blog posts from his tent overlooking Yosemite Valley.

Find the right one

Cleary, side hustles are financially beneficial; if you find the right one, it can improve your overall life satisfaction. But finding the right one can be tricky. If you don't know where to start, here is an exercise to help you brainstorm ideas for your side hustle.

1. Write out a list of things you are good at. For example, your list could include software development, project management, running, photography, and travel planning. The more things you can list out, the better. This isn't a time to be humble.
2. From that list, cross out the things you don't believe you can make money doing. Unless you're a truly elite runner, you probably won't be able to make money running, so that's off the list. But everything else seems viable enough to make some money.
3. From the remaining list, circle the things you *enjoy* doing. If you get sick of doing project management at work all day and can't imagine doing it in your free time, don't circle it.

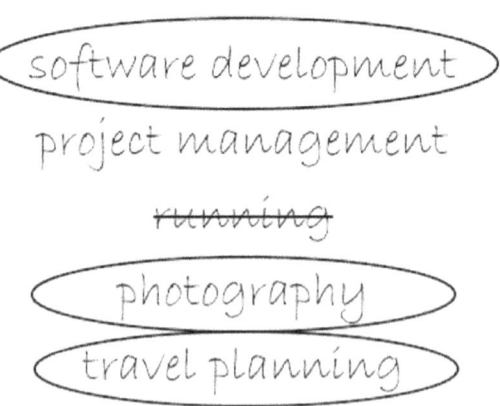

That leaves software development, photography, and travel planning as your remaining side hustle ideas. Of these, software development is the most obvious talent you can use to make money. If you have an app idea or a website you've been wanting to build, you can look to monetize those. Alternatively, you could simply do what you do in your day job, but on a freelance/consulting basis. Reach out to former employers and connections to see if they need any part-time help. If you can't drum up clients on your own, use a site like Upwork or Flexjobs to connect with companies looking to hire for contract work. This will get easier as you gain more experience and learn what you can charge for your services.

If you'd prefer to do something a bit less conventional, you could build your own small photography business. You might start by doing a couple free or discounted photoshoots for friends' events to build up a portfolio, and then ask them for referrals. Then you can decide whether to add in paid marketing and gradually build up your business to take up as much time as you're comfortable with. Unsurprisingly, I've found that the more money a side hustle makes me, the more comfortable I am spending time on it.

Travel planning might be the most difficult of the three to make money, but you could give it a try as a freelance travel planner, speaking to people about what they're looking for in a trip and then building and booking a custom itinerary perfect for them. As with the photography business, building up clients would likely be the biggest challenge. Alternatively, you could start a blog on effective travel planning and earn revenue through advertisements and affiliate links.

As a last resort for side income, if you have free time and can't think of any other way to make money, you can work as part of the "gig economy." This consists of super-short-term jobs, or gigs, that you are generally connected to through an app. Examples include driving for Uber/Lyft, making deliveries for Postmates/DoorDash, and picking up and charging those electric scooters you see strewn across the sidewalks of major cities. These are convenient because of the timing flexibility; you can work on your own schedule and earn supplemental income, even if it's only an hour at a time.

However, there are two reasons I mention these as a last resort. The first is that the gig economy is unlikely to drive success in your primary career. A good side hustle gives you skills and experience that will help you find more lucrative jobs in the future, and delivering takeout meals is unlikely to do that. The second reason is that the profit you earn will likely be small after subtracting your expenses. In the example of driving for Uber, you might earn $20 an hour or more in revenue, but you must deduct from that the additional costs you incur for insurance, tolls, gas, and maintenance to account for the wear and tear on your car. Accounting for these expenses, the average Uber driver earns just $13.70 an hour, before tax. To make an extra $10,000 a year, you would need to drive for 730 hours, about 15 hours per week. If you enjoy driving and talking to people (especially drunk people late at night), that could be a good option for you, but ensure you understand the costs before getting started.

Don't worry if your first attempt at starting a side hustle is a failure. I went through a few attempts that either didn't make money or that I really didn't enjoy before finding one that was both profitable and fulfilling. Because you're not reliant on this income to cover your expenses, it's low risk to stop or change side hustles at any time.

The key is to find your side hustle at the intersection of what you're good at, what you can make money doing, and what you enjoy. This will ensure it helps you attain your financial goals in addition to making you happy and avoiding burnout from working too much.

Make it profitable

Through my successes and failures of various side hustles, combined with the experience of dozens of others I interviewed, I have a few recommendations to ensure your side gig is financially helpful rather than harmful. First, it's important to start your side hustle by making money, not by "starting a business." Many people think of "starting a business" as coming up with a cool idea, paying $500 to form an LLC, getting friends on board as "officers" of the company, and shelling out $1,000 a month for office space at WeWork. These things are new and exciting, but unfortunately, they all *cost* money rather than *make* money

To avoid this pitfall, start off with small side hustles and experiment to see what works. You don't need to start a formal business to do this; you can simply act as a sole proprietor, the simplest form of business. A sole proprietorship is an unincorporated business with just one owner who pays personal income tax on the profits. You don't need to do anything other than to start making money to start a sole proprietorship. There is no paperwork or other official preparation.

For instance, if you like playing with dogs at the park, don't hesitate to go ahead and start a dog-walking business on the side. If you start earning substantial money or see an opportunity to increase your profit by bringing on some employees, then you can look into creating an "official" business like an LLC or corporation, which will also help protect your personal capital from the liability of the business. Guidance on creating a formal business is outside the scope of this book, but if you do go down that path, the Small Business Administration website is a great place to start.

Another action I recommend when starting a side hustle is to test the ability to make money early on. As mentioned, it can be really exciting to come up with a new idea, buy a domain, create a logo, and do the other fun aspects of starting a business. But you'd be better off spending your time and money testing your idea's profitability. This has been a challenge for me personally, as shown by the dozen unused domains I own (although I have no regrets about buying my first emoji domain, 🔥.ga). However, I have gotten better at testing profitability over time. For example, before writing a single chapter of this book, I took a page out of Tim Ferris's

4-Hour Workweek book and ran Google ads to gauge interest and land on a title.

If your side hustle sees a lot of success, you may want to scale it to become your full-time job. To minimize the risk when doing this, I recommend growing the business on the side until you earn at least enough to cover your expenses, meaning you won't be eating into your savings by quitting your day job. You should also assess how much additional income you'll be able to generate by going full-time. For example, if you went from 15 hours a week to full-time, would be you be able to find twice as many clients, or have you already saturated a small market?

If you minimize the risk of owning a business by starting it as a side hustle and accurately assessing your ability to scale, you will be well-positioned to transition into running your business full-time. This has incredible potential upside for you financially, which should be obvious when looking at the wealthiest of the wealthy: Jeff Bezos, Warren Buffett, and Bill Gates, all of whom founded their own companies and grew them to massive scale. Thus, it's not surprising that nearly half of all millionaires own a business (according to The Economist).

Matt, the millionaire electrician mentioned in the book's opening, is a great illustration of the more typical version of this upside. He started his own electrical contracting firm and increased his income from $90,000 to nearly $120,000 in just 4 years. That, combined with his investment gains, enabled him to become a millionaire at age 30. And because he was running his own business, he was able to scale back his work to 20 hours per week while still making $70,000 a year.

Matt's example shows another important benefit of side hustles that I hinted at earlier: if you find work you enjoy, you can enter semi-retirement much sooner. I'll talk more about this calculation and hitting your retirement number in Chapter 9 on financial independence, but a common rule of thumb is that you can retire when your portfolio reaches 25 times your expenses. Using that rule, if your annual expenses are $40,000, you can retire when you hit $1 million. However, if you have a side hustle you will continue in semi-retirement that earns $20,000 a year, you only need an additional $20,000 from your portfolio to fully cover your expenses. That means you can quit your day job years earlier, when you have a portfolio size of $500,000.

Ultimately, a side hustle is not *required* to become a millionaire. But earning income on the side comes with the benefits of making you more money today, driving success in your career, and helping you find your passion. When you couple that with the ability to retire much sooner, it's clear how a side hustle helps you achieve your financial goals and live the life you desire.

How I did it

While my number one key to success was undoubtedly switching companies to increase salary in my day job, my various side hustles provided a significant boost on my way to $1 million net worth. Not only did they earn me an extra $100,000 that went straight into my investment portfolio, they also helped me grow my skillset and enter new industries, contributing to my rapid salary increases in my career.

It wasn't long after I started my first "day job" of doing chores around the house for allowance that I realized I could supplement that income with other gigs. I did the typical tasks of mowing neighbors' lawns and shoveling driveways for some extra videogame money. As I got into high school, I pursued gigs that aligned a little better with my skills and interests, including jailbreaking iPhones, selling garage sale finds on eBay, and modding videogame consoles. The money I earned from each of these was negligible, but starting early helped me form a good relationship with money and understand how to earn it outside a well-defined job.

My next venture was a bit more financially significant. While in college, I started a rap music website/blog that posted the latest news, videos, album reviews, etc., earning money through Google ads. This started as a small project to test out my website building skills and write about one of my passions. As the site gained a following, I put more time into it, hired one of my friends to help me write content and ensure we were never more than an hour behind breaking news in the rap world. By the latter half of college, the ad revenue was paying for most of my apartment rent. As I transitioned to full-time work and realized I couldn't keep up with the news cycle while working a "real" job, I sold the site, netting me an extra $5,000.

Following the rap website—which I believed at the time to be a wildly successful endeavor—I fell into the trap of becoming a "scratch your own itch" entrepreneur. That is, rather than following the advice I gave you to start with a list of what you're good at and narrowing it down to what can make money, I simply did what I enjoyed and thought was cool. That worked out alright with the rap website (although my per-hour pay was not much above minimum wage), but it didn't work as well with my next idea.

"Supplemental Brewing: where your workout meets your weekend." That was the motto for the new company I founded to produce and sell protein-fortified beer. The two beers offered were Brewtein, a wheat ale packed with 7 grams of protein, and Nutribeer, a refreshing light lager with 4 grams of protein. I know this sounds ridiculous, but I'm not making this up. Here is the company logo as proof.

As a 23-year-old gym-goer and beer-drinker, I thought adding whey protein to beer was a fantastic idea, possibly the greatest invention since Reese's peanut butter cups. I was infatuated with the idea of starting a cool new business and therefore did a bunch of "cool new business" things – bought brewing equipment and t-shirts, registered an LLC, and launched a Kickstarter campaign – before I ever earned a penny in revenue.

As you might have guessed, this "business" failed. It turns out starting a brewing company is very expensive, and the market of weekend workout warriors is a pretty small niche. Supplemental Brewing shut down after only a few test batches (of questionable taste and liquid clarity) and did not generate a profit. Luckily for me, my aversion to spending money kicked in and stopped me from investing too much into it.

Ultimately, the lost money was not a big deal, but it would have been nice to spend all those hours doing something more fun and productive than scraping the label residue off hundreds of beer bottles. Despite the objective failure, Supplemental Brewing gave me some valuable experience in managing public relations and marketing. I was able to earn a few spots on news stations around the country and magazines with taglines like, "Blake Konrardy wants to start a protein beer company. He may be a renaissance man, or he may be batshit crazy." It also gave me a nice dose of business reality.

After Supplemental Brewing, I tried to mimic my past website success by creating a site to help people find an online MBA program and give them tips on how to complete it with as little time and effort as possible. But it turned out this niche wasn't big enough to generate significant revenue when people could just look at U.S. News rankings.

With a few failed ideas behind me, I finally learned to look at the intersection of what I'm good at, what can make money, and what I enjoy doing. This led me to my most successful side hustle, unsurprisingly also the closest to my day job: building predictive models for sports betting.

To find this success, I did exactly the opposite of what I did with Supplemental Brewing. I didn't create a "business" by forming an LLC and buying t-shirts. Instead, I started by assessing whether I could make money. My initial hunch was that I could use text mining and sentiment analysis to determine the public's current perception of a team and use that to help predict the team's odds of winning.

Before putting any money behind this hunch, I did months of research. I learned Python, a data science programming language I hadn't used before, and gathered data from dozens of online sources. I built predictive models and tested them in historical periods to validate that I would have been profitable in every past year I tested.

I also tested different sports to determine where I could gain an advantage. I originally tried to do baseball but found the sportsbooks' models were too accurate and already incorporated advanced data features (or at least as advanced as I was able to create). After testing a few more sports, I found my model performed the best for college basketball, for which I was able to leverage play-by-play data to create unique features that predicted whether a team would cover the spread.

After a brief ramp-up period to ensure the model was working as expected, I invested $10,000, which grew over $100,000 over the next 2 years.

This was far from a perfect system; I only won 54% of my bets and still remember my biggest loss – $35,000 on Norfolk State. But it was better than Vegas by a wide enough margin to make a lot of money. Yet despite the fact that my prediction model ran automatically every day, I was never able to put the full process on autopilot. I was constantly dealing with issues from my data sources and had to manually place all of the bets to ensure I wasn't flagged as being a bot. I brought on a couple people to help – one on the data side and one on the operations side (i.e. placing my bets for me) – which allowed me to spend more time on the model.

Besides the data issues, there was another, more challenging problem that I didn't anticipate: sportsbooks really don't like it when their customers make a profit. That means the sportsbook is losing money, and when that happens, you get kicked out. This became a major issue when I was attempting to withdraw my money from an offshore sportsbook and received a message that I needed to talk to the boss, Don. Here is how that chat went down:

Blake: Hello, I am looking to process a withdrawal and saw a message that I needed to talk to a general manager
Don: We have a pattern here
Don: I limit you
Don: You open a new account
Don: And it's happened more than once
Don: I catch you here again, I keep all the money
Don: We clear?
Blake: Yes that makes sense
Don: There will never be another warning
Don: The account will simply disappear

Luckily, Don was a man of his word, and I received my withdrawal from that account. But as you can imagine, other sportsbooks had similar feelings to Don. As I kept winning, I kept getting banned from sportsbooks – which meant that fewer and fewer would take my bets. I also had the risk of one of these books stealing my money, like Don had threatened to do. After a couple years, the risk started outweighing the reward, and I decided to move on.

As side hustles often do, my sports betting predictive modeling did more than net me an extra $100k. It also helped me land my next full-time job in Chicago with even higher pay than I had in San Francisco: as a recent expert in advanced sports data, I was the perfect fit to lead product management at a sports data company.

At this point, I was in a great financial position that allowed me to cut back on my extra work hours outside my day job. I took a break from side hustles, and instead spent more time with friends and family and enjoying watching sports instead of building predictive models for them. Nowadays, I do a bit of consulting work for a few thousand dollars of side income and have spent much of my productive time outside of work writing this book. Even if I don't make money off the book, I'll be satisfied knowing I was able to help someone reach their financial goals.

My side hustle experience has been a roller coaster of success and failure, but it was ultimately instrumental in helping me reach a $1 million net worth. This shows that not everything has to go perfectly (or even close to it) for you to attain your financial goals. If you have an idea to make money on the side, just give it a shot, minimize your risk, and you'll almost certainly end up in a better financial position.

SECTION II

Play good defense

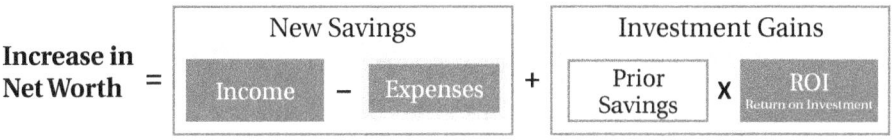

Now that we've covered how to maximize your income through your current day job, switching companies, and finding a side hustle, we can look to optimize the next component of the net worth equation: expenses.

CHAPTER 4

Reduce expenses

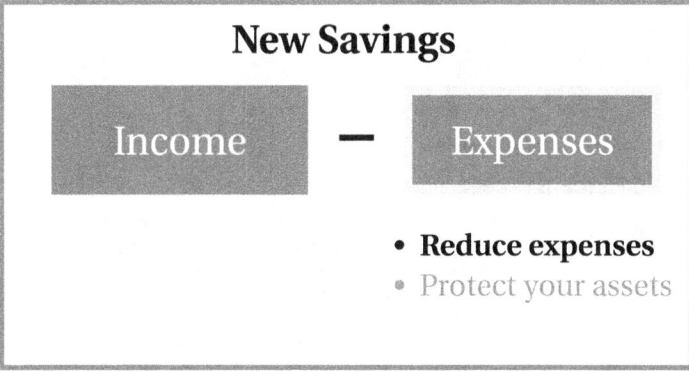

While increasing income has the greatest potential to accelerate your net worth accumulation, reducing expenses is the most efficient way to save more money.

When you earn an extra dollar of income, Uncle Sam takes his cut, equal to your marginal tax rate. So the extra dollar you earned really nets you about $0.60 that you have available to save and invest. However, a $1 reduction in expenses translates to exactly $1 more you can save and invest. And because of the power of compounding through investing, that extra dollar you saved becomes about $7.60 by the time you need it in 30 years. In this way, you can think of every dollar you save as gifting your future self $7.60. Thanks, past self!

To see the impact even a modest difference in expenses can make, let's look at an example. Remember Dave, the nurse doing IT setup as his side hustle? He has a friend, Travis, who does the same thing. Both earn the same income and investment returns. The only difference in their finances is that Travis spends a bit more.

Both Dave and Travis are busy guys between their day jobs and side gigs. To save himself some time, Travis orders in food most nights, costing him an extra $75 per week. He also hires a maid to clean his apartment every other week for $100. Neither of these expenses are extravagant by any means, but they cost him an extra $6,500 annually. Let's take a look at their finances over time.

	Dave	Travis
Primary Income	$50,000	$50,000
Side Hustle Income	$10,000	$10,000
Annual Expenses	$35,000	$41,500
Annual Saving (after taxes)	$13,000	$6,500

Net Worth		
Year	Dave	Travis
1	$13,000	$6,500
5	$88,508	$49,707
10	$255,341	$158,081
15	$543,727	$360,015
20	$1,017,082	$707,196

Even though Dave is spending just 16% less than Travis, he is able to save twice as much ($13,000 vs. $6,500 annually). This is because saving rate is not proportional to expenses. Rather, it's proportional to the **difference between income and expenses**. Travis's extra $6,500 in spending eats up half of that difference. Over time, with money invested in the market, Dave's higher saving rate enables his net worth to grow much faster. In year 20, Dave has over $1 million, over $300,000 more than Travis.

Once again, Dave is able to retire earlier than his peers. With his lower expenses and continued side income in semi-retirement, he can comfortably quit his day job after just 20 years. Travis, on the other hand, does not have enough net worth to safely quit his day job until year 25.

Essentially, Travis worked an extra 5 years of his life to pay for food delivery and a maid service. It's up to you to decide whether that is worth it. For Travis, it was not; he just didn't comprehend the impact of his expenses.

Reducing your expenses doesn't have to mean living a less fulfilling life. Quite the contrary, knowing where your money is going and being intentional about spending it can make people significantly happier. Based on a survey from Ally Bank, people who save money report being 30% happier than those who spend it all instead. Having a sense of financial security and making progress toward long-term financial goals provides a sense of fulfillment that spending doesn't grant.

You can effectively balance saving and spending by adopting a practical outlook on money and recognizing that it is not a sacred object you can't part ways with. Rather, as I've emphasized throughout this book, money is a *tool* to help get what you want in life. By effectively prioritizing your expenses, you can spend money on the things that make you happy while also quickly growing your net worth. To do so, you must make conscious cost-benefit decisions between spending a dollar today and gifting your future self $7.60.

With or without a budget

You can effectively reduce your expenses either with or without a budget. Either way, the goal is to consciously choose what to spend on. Personally, I don't use a budget, but I have seen them be a huge help to many others, so I'll cover both methods—starting with creating a budget.

With a budget

As mentioned, your goal is to consciously choose what you spend money on by analyzing the benefits of what you get vs. what you're giving up (money now and even more money in the future). In economic terms, this is a cost-benefit analysis. But doing that analysis sounds like a bit of overkill when you're deciding whether it's worth it to add bacon to your cheeseburger.

That is the purpose of budgets: to help simplify these small decisions. Budgets are essentially a way of batch-processing the spending decisions you will need to make over the course of a year so that you don't need to make these decisions in daily life.

When creating a budget, the first input you will need is your income: how much you have available to spend. For this purpose, you should ensure you're using after-tax income. I've spoken with far too many people who get a $5,000 promotion and start thinking where the extra $5k will go. About $2,000 of that will go straight to the U.S. government, so your planning should start with $3,000. Your tax rate will vary based on your income and how much you leverage tax-advantaged investment accounts, which are discussed in detail later. To get a good estimate of taxes, you can use this income tax calculator from Smart Asset.

Once your income is set, it's now time to allocate that money, and the best place to start is to pay yourself first. This means starting your budget by allocating the amount you want to be saving and working from there to see how much you can afford in different spending categories. This "pay yourself first" mindset is easy to implement in practice using automated investing through your company's payroll or your brokerage company. You can simply set up an amount to be deposited from each paycheck, and you'll never even see the money as available to spend.

Next, you'll want to fill in the big recurring expenses for housing, food, transportation, insurance, and childcare. Typically, these categories will cover over 80% of your spending, so it's worth spending more time on them rather than worrying about whether to buy brand-name dish soap. I'll provide some tips to reduce spending in each of these categories later in this chapter.

After adding these big expenses, you can fill in the remaining smaller expenses like household items. To avoid going down the rabbit hole of estimating how many lightbulbs you'll go through next year, it's best to look back at your total spending in this category last year and use that as a starting point.

Now that you've covered all necessary spending, it's time to see what's left for additional saving and discretionary spending. This is where you make the decision whether you can fit in Starbucks five times a week and if that's more important to you than an annual vacation or saving extra. Also, this is the point where you may find that your budget is now negative. In that case, you need to reconsider whether you can cut back on any previously allocated expenses, starting with the largest ones, or whether you must reduce your goal saving rate.

The above advice assumes you have a decent grasp on your spending. If that's the case, you can follow these steps with a simple spreadsheet. However, if you're starting out with no clue where your money is going, you may need some help creating a budget. In that case, I recommend trying out YNAB (You Need A Budget), which will guide you step-by-step.

Without a budget

As previously mentioned, budgets are beneficial for people who want to simplify their spending decisions. That's a great way to start, but if you want to be a millionaire, you need to have a good relationship with money and be able to make these decisions without getting stressed. Remember, money is merely a tool to help get what you want in life. And I've never met a craftsman who is afraid of his toolset.

This is why I do not use a budget but instead make conscious decisions about what I want to buy based on what I believe will truly increase my life satisfaction. I view spending money as an exercise in life prioritization: would I rather buy that thing now or be able to retire a bit earlier? When you start to look at spending this way, you don't need a budget. Instead, it becomes a personal challenge to see how much you can save rather than a predetermined number.

You might be thinking something like, "well if my employer needs a budget, then surely *I* do." One reason big companies require budgets is that employees have conflicting interests. Marketing always wants to spend more on advertisements, and everyone wants their department to hire more employees to reduce their individual workload. However, when you're making money decisions for your own life, you naturally look out for your own interests and don't need the artificial limit that comes with a budget. These artificial limits eliminate the challenge of saving as much as possible and can create a mindset of "well I have $300 left in the budget this month, might as well buy a couple new golf clubs."

This budget-less method of conscious prioritization works great for me, which is unsurprising since prioritization is a huge part of my day job as a product manager. This has helped me discern which things *don't* actually make me happy—for example cable and Netflix subscriptions—so I stopped spending money on them. At the same time, I was able to prioritize spending on new experiences, such as exploring the Japanese island of Ishigaki and buying a Vespa to scoot around Chicago.

To be clear, not using a budget still requires regular monitoring to see where your money is going. This is necessary to determine whether you are spending on the right priorities and look for ways to increase your saving rate. The only difference is that without a budget you will not have hard limits, and instead will need to make more decisions as you go.

Now that we've covered a couple methods to track and allocate spending, let's move on to the details of cutting down your spending in practice. The rest of this chapter will focus on strategies to reduce specific expense categories that often have significant room for improvement. But first, an overarching spending tip: reduce the number of things you buy and instead use that money for experiences that make you truly happy. That can mean experiences you buy today such as travel or experiences in the future obtained by saving. The ultimate example of this is early retirement, which allows you to spend your time on whatever you desire.

Harvard researcher Daniel Gilbert et al. distilled the results of various money-happiness studies and concluded that "if money doesn't make you happy then you probably aren't spending it right." By making smarter spending decisions and buying fewer things, you'll not only have more money to save, you'll also increase your happiness.

Gilbert's research shows that the vast majority of people derive greater happiness from experiential purchases and view them as more self-defining than their material purchases. This is because people tend to overestimate the happiness they'll get from things like a new car or a remodeled kitchen. Sure, those marble countertops look great and give you a rush when you enter the kitchen for the first week, but over time, they blend into the background of life. Experiences, on the other hand, tend to provide lasting value over time. For example, when spending money on travel, you get excitement and anticipation from planning the trip, enjoyment during the trip itself, and countless stories (and photos) you can recount with friends and family for years to come.

Another important finding from this study is that spending money on others is effective at increasing happiness. This is a result of innate altruism (it feels good to help others) as well as the comfort of being with those you care about. When determining your spending, ensure you prioritize spending time with your favorite people, friends and family.

A final tip to maximize your happiness from your spending: buy more frequent small pleasures rather than infrequent big purchases. As I mentioned earlier, you will get used to the new car and remodeled kitchen after a short time – to the extent they'll no longer bring you happiness. Spending on small pleasures helps fight this adaptation and keep things interesting. So, don't hesitate to buy yourself some nice wool socks, spend $20 to go to the local minor league baseball game, or join a bowling league with your buddies. Research shows those things will make you happy without breaking the bank.

In summary, you can maximize your happiness given the money you have available by optimizing your spending. Generally, this means spending less on things and more on experiences. You can also increase your life satisfaction by saving $1 today and gifting your future self $7.60, enabling an earlier retirement. To help you save that extra $1 today, let's look at some specific tips in the most significant spending categories.

Housing

The average American spends 37% of their after-tax income on housing, more than any other expense. By optimizing your housing spend, you can substantially increase your saving rate and grow your net worth.

People often make a big mistake in this category by letting their income dictate their housing expense. "How much house can I afford?" is commonly asked on financial forums, and various rules of thumb exist. For example, you'll hear that 30% of pretax income is an acceptable allowance for your housing spend. This mindset does not work if you want to accumulate wealth quickly. If you follow a percentage-based rule of thumb, your housing expense will grow proportionally with your income, when you could instead put that newfound income toward additional saving and investing. So rather than seeking housing based on a percentage of income, the key is to determine what aspects are important to you and find the lowest-cost living arrangement that meets those criteria.

If you want to see examples of people getting creative to reduce their housing expense, look no further than San Francisco, where crazy high rents drive people to "unique" housing situations. I have one friend who lived in what was essentially a hostel, with a bunk bed and a dresser drawer as the only spaces he could call his own. Another friend lived in his van parked at the company office and showered at the gym. Both of them were able to save thousands each month by minimizing their housing expenses. But if you're like me and would prefer being able to stand upright in your home and get a proper shower, don't worry; there are less-extreme ways to save.

Before discussing how to make cuts to your housing expense, I want to mention one aspect you should not neglect – location. As mentioned in the income section of this book, living in a certain region can earn you up to double the income for doing exactly the same job. Yes, your expenses will be higher, but likely not enough to negate the higher salary. So, don't rule out areas of the country simply because they have a higher cost of living.

Looking at location more granularly, you should also seek a home close to your workplace. Keeping a short commute enables you to excel in your day job while also having time to earn additional income through a side hustle. If your commute is a short walk rather than a 45-minute drive each way, that's an extra 7.5 hours per week—equivalent to one full workday—that you have available to work on your side hustle. Greater success in your day job and your side hustle will likely more than compensate for any additional costs to live close to work. You also realize direct cost savings through spending less on gas, tolls, car maintenance, parking, and more (additional detail on transportation expenses coming in the next section). And on a non-financial note, a short commute gives you more time to do what you enjoy in life. I know this is a financial book, but that's a pretty big benefit.

Given the above, location is the most important aspect to consider when looking for a new place—and you shouldn't choose an unideal location just for cost savings. Instead, there are many other aspects of housing on which you can compromise to substantially reduce your expenses. Here are some general tips that apply whether you are renting or own your home.

1. Don't buy more house than you need

If you're renting, it obviously costs more to get a 1200 square foot 3-bedroom apartment than a 600 square foot 1-bedroom. But even if you own, recurring expenses like mortgage interest, property tax, utilities, and insurance are all higher for larger homes. In addition to saving money directly, having a smaller home also provides an incentive not to buy expensive furniture and other material things just to fill your house, thereby reducing spending in other categories. And you have less to clean!

2. Live with roommates

Across the 25 largest U.S. cities, 2-bedroom apartments cost 25% more on average than 1-bedroom apartments (according to Rent Café). If you can find a roommate that you get along with and split a 2-bedroom rather than living alone, you'll cut your housing expense by 37%. For example, if you would pay $1,000 for a 1-bedroom apartment in your area, you and a roommate would be able to split the cost of a $1,250 2-bedroom apartment, paying just $625 each. That's an extra $4,500 you can save every year. Over the course of 10 years, that extra savings coupled with 7% returns gives you an additional $62,000 in net worth.

This idea also applies if you own your home. In that case, you can look to rent out any extra bedrooms year-round or list them on Airbnb. This will be a bit more work to take on the role of a landlord, but the financial upside is also higher – you may be able to pay your entire mortgage from your additional revenue, essentially paying $0 net for housing. Scott at Millennial Money calls this "house hacking." Clearly, paying essentially nothing for housing will greatly accelerate your savings.

3. Don't splurge on frills

Remember the principle mentioned at the start of this chapter: buying nicer material things typically does not lead to increased long-term happiness. That has been scientifically proven. That means it's probably not worth it to splurge on marble countertops, stainless steel appliances, and other nice finishes. They will look good for a few weeks before fading into the background of life. This is especially true for rental units, where an increasing number of apartments are being framed as "luxury units" with 50% higher rents for no real benefit.

Additionally, if you're handy, you can save by getting a place that needs some restoration work. When looking at real estate brokerage site Redfin for the Chicago area, it's common to see houses that were bought for under $250,000, had the interior renovated, then sold for $375,000 eight months later. This definitely isn't for everyone, including me, a guy who gave up on repairing a drywall hole as soon as the wikiHow page said to take out my "carpenter's square." But if you're comfortable putting some labor and a small financial investment into your home, you'll reduce your living cost and increase the value of your home when you eventually sell it.

4. Do your research

Finding a place that meets your location requirements and all the other criteria above takes time. You will need to get a sense of the market to understand what a good value looks like. To do this, spend some time on Craigslist, Trulia, Redfin, Zillow, and any local listing sites to understand the tradeoffs you can make in return for a lower rent/mortgage payment. These sites have filters to make that convenient. Do you need a washer/dryer in-unit or is one in the building okay? Do you need a balcony, or can you hang out in the shared patio and yard? After a few hours of browsing and noting the best options currently on the market, you'll be able to identify deals as they become available and move quickly to snag them.

Regardless of if you're renting or buying, be sure to leverage the negotiation techniques covered in the income section to negotiate a lower rent or purchase price. As mentioned before, the best negotiation tactic is to have other options and play them against each other. You can be even more aggressive using that technique to negotiate housing, since you don't have to worry about losing your job if you rub someone the wrong way. For example, you can say "this other apartment complex has comparable amenities and a price of $x for a 2-bedroom. Can you match that?" I used this to get rent below the asking price at every place I have lived, including during lease renewal. At one apartment, I was even able to negotiate a lower rent in my second year living there.

The advice up to this point has been universal, regardless of whether you rent or own your home. Now it's time to address the age-old question:

Should you rent, or should you buy?

If you're looking for a longer-term housing solution, buying a house that you expect to live in for several years can be a great investment to reduce your future expenses. However, buying a house can also be a financial trap to spending way more on housing than you would otherwise. Before getting into the detailed calculations, here are some bad reasons to own a house that I commonly hear, along with simple rebuttals.

I hate throwing my money away on rent. I'd rather put money toward owning a home.

Owning a home is not free; you have ongoing expenses of mortgage interest, property taxes, insurance, and maintenance that are all "throwing money away" just as much as paying rent. Plus, there are substantial transaction costs associated with buying or selling a house (shown in more detail below).

I need a 4-bedroom house because I plan to have 3 kids in the future.

It's unwise to assume you know your exact needs 10 years from now. What if you don't have children or decide to stop at one or two? Instead, you can rent a smaller place for much cheaper until you actually *do* need the bigger home.

I'm only expecting to live in it for a couple years, but I can probably rent it out after that.

If you only live in your house for a couple of years, you'll be eaten alive by the transaction costs of buying and selling your house. Also, you cannot expect owning property to be passive income like investing is. Just like the stock market, housing prices can go up and down, impacting your ability to make a good profit renting. Unlike the stock market, you may have to go to your house in the middle of the night to deal with a burst pipe. No matter how much Amazon stock you own, I promise Jeff Bezos isn't going to call you in the middle of the night.

While the above are all bad reasons to own a home, there are good reasons, too. Purchasing a house can be a great financial decision. However, it will be the most expensive purchase you ever make (unless you have some *very* expensive hobbies like yachting), so it's worth going through the math in detail. When doing so, you may be shocked at how long it takes for you to come out ahead vs. renting. As a general rule, the longer you will live in your house, the more it makes sense to buy, with a breakeven point typically between 5 and 10 years. Here are the factors that must be considered when performing this calculation:

- **Transaction costs** of buying and selling a home. Typically, buyers will need to pay mortgage closing costs of about 3% of their home purchase price, and sellers will pay a broker fee of around 6%. This is the main reason why buying a house does not make financial sense unless you plan to live there for several years.
- **Recurring expenses**. When renting, your recurring expenses are nearly 100% known and fixed. When buying a home, the costs are more hidden but include the interest

you pay on your mortgage, property taxes, homeowners insurance, and maintenance/repair costs, which can be difficult to estimate and tend to occur in spurts.
- **Home ownership tax benefits.** You may have heard that there are tax advantages for owning a home. That is true, but likely not for the reason you expect. Previously, most homeowners took advantage of the mortgage interest deduction, allowing them to deduct any mortgage interest payments from their taxable income. However, the Tax Cuts and Jobs Act of 2018 reduced the limits and nearly doubled the standard deduction, meaning that the more than 70% of Americans who do not itemize their deductions see no benefit. Instead, the biggest tax advantage of home ownership is the capital gains exemption, which makes a portion of your gains when selling a home tax-free. This won't benefit you in the short-term but can be a big benefit if you sell your home many years in the future for a significantly higher price than you paid.
- **Opportunity cost** of a down payment. This is the most often-neglected cost of buying a home. For a $300,000 house, that $60,000 down payment could instead be invested in the market. Over very long time periods, the stock market has returned real (adjusted for inflation) gains of about 7%, while single-family homes have appreciated less than 1% annually.

With those factors in mind, let's calculate an example comparing two families: the Renters and the Owners.

Two recently married couples currently live in one-bedroom apartments in a large, medium cost-of-living city. Both couples have an investment portfolio of $100,000 and plan on having kids in the next few years. After subtracting other expenses, both have $50,000 available each year to spend on housing. They save any amount they do not spend as part of their investment portfolio.

Here is a timeline summarizing the major life events for both families.

Year 1: both couples would like to start having kids within the next two years. In anticipation of this life event, the Owners decide to buy a 3-bedroom house, while the Renters continue renting a 1-bedroom apartment.

Year 2: both couples have their first child. The renters move into a 2-bedroom apartment to have a separate room for the baby.

Year 5: both couples have their second child. With two kids and their oldest approaching school age, the Owners decide to sell their house and buy in a more desirable area with better schools. The Renters move to a 3-bedroom house in the same area, continuing to rent their home.

Year 6 and beyond: both families stay in their homes and raise their two children. The Owners gradually pay off their mortgage, and the Renters continue to pay monthly rent.

Here is a year-by-year breakdown of how these two families fared financially.

Renters	
First rental monthly rent	$1,900
Second rental monthly rent	$2,400
Third rental monthly rent	$3,250

Owners	
First home price	$325,000
Second home price	$400,000
Home buying costs	4% of purchase price
Home selling costs	6% of purchase price
Down payment	20%
Mortgage interest	4%

	Renters		Owners			
Year	Housing Expense	Net Worth	Housing Expense	Investment Portfolio	Home Equity	Total Net Worth
0	-	$ 100,000	-	$ 100,000	-	100,000
1	$ 23,000	$ 134,000	$ 106,000	$ 44,000	$ 70,000	$ 114,000
2	$ 29,000	$ 165,000	$ 28,000	$ 68,000	$ 77,000	$ 145,000
3	$ 30,000	$ 199,000	$ 28,000	$ 95,000	$ 85,000	$ 180,000
4	$ 31,000	$ 237,000	$ 29,000	$ 125,000	$ 93,000	$ 218,000
5	$ 42,000	$ 267,000	$ 81,000	$ 102,000	$100,000	$ 202,000
6	$ 43,000	$ 299,000	$ 37,000	$ 127,000	$110,000	$ 237,000
7	$ 44,000	$ 334,000	$ 37,000	$ 154,000	$121,000	$ 275,000
8	$ 45,000	$ 373,000	$ 38,000	$ 184,000	$133,000	$ 317,000
9	$ 46,000	$ 415,000	$ 38,000	$ 218,000	$146,000	$ 364,000
10	$ 47,000	$ 461,000	$ 39,000	$ 254,000	$159,000	$ 413,000
15	$ 51,000	$ 767,000	$ 42,000	$ 504,000	$245,000	$ 749,000
20	$ 57,000	$ 1,242,000	$ 46,000	$ 904,000	$369,000	$ 1,273,000
25	$ 63,000	$ 1,981,000	$ 50,000	$ 1,536,000	$549,000	$ 2,085,000
30	$ 69,000	$ 3,124,000	$ 56,000	$ 2,525,000	$770,000	$ 3,295,000

You can see how much the transaction costs of buying and selling a home erode the Owners' net worth accumulation in their early years. At year 5, the Renters are $65,000 ahead in net worth. Looking at years 6 and beyond, you can see that the Owners have a lower housing expense each year, but it takes a long time to make up for the lost investment gains.

However, the Owners end up substantially ahead after staying in the same home for 25 years. At year 30, they have a net worth $170,000 higher than the Renters, although both end up in fantastic financial positions because of their saving rate and investment performance.

Analyzing this example, neither family optimized their housing costs. The optimal route would be renting until year 5, purchasing the 3-bedroom house, and living in that house for another 25 years. Unfortunately, life can be hard to predict, so taking a truly optimal path is unlikely. In short, if you think you might need to move in the next 5 years, it is typically financially advantageous to rent, though you should do the math for your situation to check.

If you don't want to run the numbers by hand, I don't blame you. This calculation is the most complex you'll see in this book. Luckily, the New York Times rent vs. buy calculator provides a solid approximation. The default values it uses are a bit pessimistic for investment returns (assuming you follow the advice of this book), so you'll want to increase that value. Also, ensure you are realistic about how long you will stay in a house. People like to think the home they are buying is their "forever home," but the reality is that most first-time home buyers will move in less than 12 years.

I may seem from all these warnings to be anti-homeownership. However, I don't want to downplay the upsides of owning. Using our example above, it's clear you can come out way ahead financially if you plan to own your house for a long time. Additionally, if you're nearing retirement, having a paid-off house reduces the risk that you won't be able to cover your expenses. In essence, buying a house is spending money up-front to reduce and stabilize your ongoing annual expenses.

There are also non-financial aspects to consider with regards to housing. According to the Bogleheads wiki, "There is no definitive answer for owning vs. renting a home. There can be a financial answer as to whether it is cheaper to buy or rent. However, other considerations such as emotional, environmental, and flexibility can sometimes outweigh decisions that may not be financially justified." To that point, owning a house may provide a lifestyle that is something not possible with renting. For example, if you're handy and like doing significant renovations, you should own a home. If you like moving around every few years, you should rent.

If you have no preference otherwise and are simply focused on accumulating wealth, keep in mind that increasing income as quickly as possible may require changing jobs every couple years. Even if you do this within the same area, a new job could double your commute time. Renting thus gives you more flexibility to switch to new jobs and move closer to them.

Housing will likely be your biggest expense over the course of your life, so it's worth real effort to optimize it. Because location is so important to your life satisfaction and your financial success, I don't recommend cutting costs there, but instead looking at home size, finishes, and whether you can live with a roommate. There is no definitive answer for whether renting vs. buying is preferable; you'll need to run the numbers for your personal situation. However, unless you plan to live in the same house for several years, you'll come out ahead financially by renting.

Transportation

After housing, transportation provides the greatest opportunity to cut costs and increase your saving rate. Many people subconsciously overspend in this category because the total cost isn't as obvious as rent or a mortgage payment. For example, I know couples living in downtown Chicago, which has plenty of public transit options, who own 2 cars and Uber to bars or friends' places every week. I'm sure they would be shocked if they added up their total transportation expense in a year.

Unsurprisingly, the number one way to cut your transportation cost is to reduce your car ownership. Owning a car is expensive. According to AAA, the average American spends $8,900 per year to own a car when including costs such as depreciation, maintenance, fuel, and insurance. Adding in $200 per month for parking in a major city brings the total cost to $11,500 per year.

Knowing that expense, consider if you need to own a car. If you're living in a city, could you take public transportation or bike? Compared to the costs of owning a car, these are basically free. Even if ditching your car would mean moving closer to work and cost you an extra $500 per month, you'd come out well ahead. Also, if you just need a car once in a while, paying for occasional car usage is easier than ever with Uber/Lyft and car sharing services like Zipcar, Turo, and Getaround. I can typically find cars for a full day rental for under $30.

If you can't ditch car ownership altogether, see if you can reduce your number of cars. If you're living with a partner, could you share one car? And does any household really need three or four cars?

Rachel and I asked ourselves this question when we moved from central Illinois to San Francisco. We estimated that our total cost to own a car there would be about $12,000 annually. Rather than moving with both of our cars, we decided to sell one. We lived just over a mile from my work, so I was able to walk, and Rachel drove to work every day. If I needed to get around while Rachel had the car, I took public transportation or Uber. We spent about $500 on transit in our first year there. That means by selling our car, we saved $11,500 each year. Making that decision over the course of 30 years of driving, compounding for investment returns, results in a **$1.1 million difference**.

I grew up in small towns, so I recognize that you simply need a car to get around in most places in the U.S. But even then, you can take steps to drastically reduce the cost of car ownership – chiefly, buying sensible, lower-cost cars and owning them for a long time.

A good example of this comes from Taylor Larimore, financial expert and "The Dean of the Vanguard Diehards." Taylor noticed that his neighbor bought a new BMW right around the same time he bought a new Toyota Corolla. Taylor obviously made the more frugal choice; his car cost $19,000 new while his neighbor's was $58,000. But the purchase price is just the up-front cost. What about ongoing cost of ownership? What if they repeated that buying behavior over the course of their driving lives, from age 25 to 65? And what if Taylor took the money he saved on car expenses and invested it in the market instead? Considering all of these factors to calculate the total cost of ownership, Taylor saves an extra $9,000 per year compared to his neighbor. That extra $9,000 each year for 30 years, when invested in the market, is a difference of over $850,000.

Similar to the tip I provided for housing, you're best off financially buying the smallest car that suites your needs without any frills. If you can make do with a small sedan, total ownership will cost you $6,400 per year on average, while a pickup truck costs over $10,000.

When buying a new car, many financial experts recommend buying used to let the first owner take the big depreciation hit when driving it off the lot. However, this has changed in the past couple decades, and there is no longer much of a premium for buying new. If you prefer to buy new cars, you should be able to justify that financially as long as you keep the car for longer and spread out the depreciation over many years.

Many experts also recommend avoiding car loans and paying cash instead. If you're following the advice of this book and are growing your portfolio, you'll easily be able to do that, and it's never a bad decision. But if you have a solid credit score, you may get a great deal on an auto loan. If you can get a loan at 2% interest or less, feel free to take that and invest the extra money in the market. Your investment returns will likely be greater than the low interest rate on your loan, so you'll come out ahead.

Food and drink

How you spend money on food is a lifestyle choice that can make a big impact on your saving rate. Buying a coffee at Starbucks every morning for $4 and a $10 lunch at Chipotle seems fairly harmless when you think about it as $14 a day. However, if you made coffee at home and brought your lunch to work instead, that would only cost you about $3. This $11 difference per day, added across every weekday over a 30-year career, would be worth $270,000 if invested instead.

You can choose which you'd rather have: daily Starbucks and Chipotle or $270,000.

If you chose the $270,000, the best place to start is at the grocery store so you can make meals at home as often as possible. There really is no substitute that comes close to this in terms of cost. Forbes recently compared the cost of preparing meals with grocery store food, cooking a prepared meal kit (from a company like Blue Apron or Home Chef), and ordering restaurant delivery. The average cost of a meal cooked at home was $4.31, a meal kit almost triple that at $12.41, and restaurant delivery nearly 5 times the cost at $20.37.

Because of this significant difference in cost, even small changes to your eating habits can save you a lot of money. If you currently grab takeout or order in 5 times per week and spend $100, cutting that to 2 times per week will save you about $47, factoring in the additional $13 grocery cost. $47 extra every week is $2,444 per year that you can save and invest. That difference over the course of 30 years adds over $230,000 to your net worth, simply by ordering food less often.

Clearly, eating restaurant food is expensive. But that doesn't mean you're left to choose between eating ramen every meal or spending an hour a day cooking in order to save money. Here are some tips to help you save while still enjoying your meals.

- **Prepare your own breakfast and lunch**. For most people, these meals are part of a daily routine and less about enjoying the experience compared to dinner, so they're a great place to save money. As shown in the Starbucks and Chipotle example, a simple coffee and lunch every day could end up costing you nearly $300,000. Instead, grab some fruit/yogurt/breakfast bars from the store, bring your lunch to work, and take advantage of any free coffee and food or snacks you might have at your office.
- **Prepare bulk meals in advance**. Most people don't want to spend an hour every day cooking. Luckily, you don't have to in order to eat homemade meals. Rachel and I (meaning 95% Rachel) prepare lunches for the week on Sunday, usually making a big casserole that includes some combination of pasta, meat, cheese, and veggies. We'll also mix and match dishes throughout the week, such as grilling a couple pounds of chicken to eat in tacos, with pasta, on a

sandwich, etc. In total, these bulk dishes cost about $15 to cover all my lunches for the week. We'll often use bulk meals to cover our lunches and some of our weekday dinners, saving our more creative culinary endeavors for the weekends.

- **Avoid expensive alcohol**. While not drinking alcohol is a surefire way to save money, I don't have the gall to ask that of you, especially since I drink my fair share (and a couple extra fair shares too). However, you can save by sticking to cheaper brands, not being swayed by labels or assuming that higher price points mean better quality. Instead, try a blind taste test to see what you actually like and whether a cheap alternative is sufficient. One study showed that even sommeliers, people who taste wine for a living, can't tell a red from a white with added food coloring—proving that appearances can be deceiving.
- **Make eating out or going to the bar an event rather than an expectation**. This is a psychological change that will save you more than any other food tip. As with other categories, routine spending on restaurants causes the novelty to fade, no longer bringing you excitement. If you reserve going out for special events, you'll save a lot of money and more thoroughly enjoy your occasional visit to a restaurant or bar.
- **Look for ways to save when eating out**. If you truly enjoy eating out at restaurants, you don't have to stop completely to reduce your spending. For example, alcohol and soft drinks are priced at a huge markup, so consider sticking to water and having a couple glasses of wine when you get home. You can also look for days or times with special deals or happy hours so you can get the same food and experience at a lower price.
- **Go to places you enjoy, not places you are *supposed* to enjoy**. You can easily spend hundreds or thousands at

restaurants eating escargot and caviar or the surf-and-turf dinner. But consider whether those places actually bring you the most enjoyment. They do not for me, which is why I drag Rachel to Taco Bell every year to celebrate my birthday.

- **Last but not least, keep your freezer stocked with an emergency frozen pizza or some leftovers you can heat up in the microwave.** Regardless of how well you meal prep, there will be times things don't go according to plan. Some recent personal examples include when I decided 0-degree weather is too cold for me to grill or when I got back from a flight at 10pm and had nothing in the fridge. In these cases, having a quick, easy meal available, like a $4 frozen pizza or something similar, will save you from spending money ordering food.

Childcare and education

Having children is expensive. Regardless of how frugal you are, there is no way around that. However, there are a few key decisions I'll highlight that can lessen the financial blow of raising a family.

The first major expense you'll likely incur (after the hospital bills, which I'll touch on in the insurance section in Chapter 5), is childcare. To be frank, childcare costs a ton. The average annual cost of daycare in my state of Illinois is $13,500 in 2020, and unless you know someone who runs a daycare, there aren't any great tips to save. But there *are* some alternatives you should consider.

Because daycare is so expensive, it may be worthwhile for one parent to stay at home if you have multiple daycare-age children. Let's look at an example with 2 kids. On average, annual daycare costs would total $27,000. About $1,200 of that is offset by a dependent care tax credit. Here is the financial breakdown when one parent earns $80,000 and the other earns $40,000.

	Both Parents Working	One Parent Stay at Home
Salary	$120,000	$80,000
After Tax Income	$92,356	$63,861
Day Care Expense	$27,000	-
Tax Credit	$1,200	-
Remaining Income	**$66,556**	**$63,861**

As this shows, the decision for the lower-earning spouse to keep working or to stay home with the kids is nearly breakeven. The difference of $2,700 may be quite a bargain for the quality of life improvement. Ultimately, it comes down to parenting preferences, but it is worth doing the math to make an informed financial decision.

Once your kids surpass daycare age, there is another key financial decision to be made: private school or public school. The average private school tuition is about $8,000 per year. Assuming 2 kids with 13 years of private school each, the total cost is $208,000. Factoring in the opportunity cost from investing that money over a 30-year period, the true cost is close to $900,000. Clearly, it is financially advantageous for you to send your kids to public school, even if that means moving to a new neighborhood where you are more comfortable with the public school (and where property taxes might be higher).

I recognize there are many non-financial factors in that decision, and I'm not going to spend a chapter trying to convince you that public schools are better. Research has shown that private school students *do* perform better than their public-school peers. However, channeling my background as a statistician, it's important to remember that correlation does not equal causation. The performance gap between public and private schools is eliminated when controlling for socioeconomic factors (according to a University of Virginia study). This means private school students do better because their parents are financially stable and actively engaged in their lives; the school experience itself seems to make little difference. Based on those research findings, I will have no hesitations sending my kids to public school and enjoying the significant savings.

One final decision I'll mention when it comes to raising children is funding college. Parents have differing viewpoints on whether they should contribute to their children's college expenses. This is a big financial decision, as you need to balance helping your child start their adult life in a good position without ruining your retirement funding.

I will not opine on that decision, but if you do choose to help fund college, I recommend leveraging a 529 savings plan, which allows you to reduce your taxable income in most states. This is discussed in more detail in the investing section. When funding this account, consider covering the equivalent of your state university's tuition, allowing your children to pay the difference if they decide to go somewhere more expensive. Hopefully they'll turn out financially responsible like their parents!

Debt, credit cards, and other expenses

Avoid bad debt

Having debt is not inherently a bad thing; it just means you are borrowing money. Mortgages and student loans are examples of debt that can be financially advantageous in the long run. However, most types of debt are a net negative on your finances, and some are a downright financial disaster. To keep your expenses in check, you'll need to eliminate and avoid bad debt.

I said up front that there are no mandates in this book. That wasn't entirely true, because this is the one mandate: pay off all your credit card debt now.

The average household has over $8,000 in credit card debt. If they make the minimum monthly payment of $160 and are charged an average interest rate of 18.9%, it will take them 8 years to pay it off—and that does not include any additional purchases. By that time, they will have paid $7,000 in interest, meaning they spent $15,000 to buy $8,000 worth of stuff. You don't have to be a financial genius to recognize that paying double the purchase price is a bad move. And that extra expense doesn't even include the opportunity cost of investing. Once we factor this in, if you spend $1,000 in credit card interest payments each year (close to the average household value) for 30 years, you will lose out on nearly $100,000 of net worth.

This shows why having even small amounts of credit card debt should be considered a financial emergency that you must address ASAP. If you have credit card debt, you probably don't have extra cash sitting around, but you should do whatever it takes to save and pay it off quickly. If that means you need to eat ramen for the next month, that's what you should do. As motivation, recognize that you will never have a better investment opportunity, since your return is equal to your interest rate of around 19%.

This advice applies to other short-term debt such as payday loans or anything else approaching double-digit interest rates. Beyond these financial emergencies, you should consider paying down debt early to be part of your investment strategy, and you will need to determine whether it is more beneficial than investing in the market. For example, should you pay off your student loans at 5.6% or save more in your 401k? This will be covered in the investing chapters later in this book (Put your money in the right spot).

Use credit cards intelligently

Now that we've seen the downsides of credit cards, let's talk about the upsides and why nearly all my spending is done using a credit card. By using credit cards intelligently (not just responsibly), you can significantly reduce your expenses.

Credit cards get a bad rap in financial circles, deservedly so given how insane the interest rates are. But that doesn't mean you should swear them off. Responsible use of credit cards costs no more than a debit card; just don't spend what you don't have available in your checking account and you can pay it off in full each month to avoid interest payments. This will also help you build a good credit score, which can save you a ton of money on a mortgage or car loan.

While responsible use of credit cards is good, intelligent use of credit cards is even better. By using credit cards with rewards points, you'll earn money just for spending what you would have anyway.

Much of my travel has been funded partially or entirely through credit card rewards. If you like to travel, consider what airline or hotel chain you normally use and check if they offer a credit card with a large sign-up bonus. If you don't have preferred travel companies, you can also go with a general travel card, such as the Chase Sapphire Reserve. When I signed up for this card in 2016, I got a 100,000-point welcome bonus, with each point redeemable for 1.5 cents in travel credit. That's $1,500 in free travel, enough for a trip to Europe, without making any changes to my spending.

One tip to accumulate points quickly: if you travel for work, see if you can use your own card and get reimbursed rather than using a company credit card. This will allow you to rack up your individual points while spending company money. Another perk of work travel is that you can often tack your own personal travel onto it to reduce your personal expenses while exploring the world. Flying to NY for a business meeting? Check if you can book your flight back on Sunday and spend the weekend there for only the cost of two hotel nights (which you will probably be able to cover with points).

Travel cards often provide the best dollar value on spending since they offer higher redemption rates with their travel partners. However, if you don't travel much, a percentage cash back is likely the best choice for you. It is the simplest approach, crediting your account with cash each month that you can spend on whatever you want.

Regardless of how you spend, it's worth doing some research on current deals, since they're constantly changing. The Points Guy is the renowned authority on reward credit cards, so check there to determine what card is best for you.

Clearly, reward credit cards have some great benefits, but don't fall into the trap of buying something just to earn extra points. Just because Apple is running a promotion to give you 6% back on holiday spending with the Apple card doesn't mean you suddenly need a $250 pair of AirPods. Apple wants you to believe you're saving $15, when in reality you're spending $235 that you wouldn't have otherwise spent.

Travel on the cheap

Assuming you can't cover all of your travel expenses with points, here are some more tips to keep your spending low.

- **Be flexible with your travel dates and times**. By traveling during non-peak times, you can often save 70% or more on flights and hotels. And if you're super flexible and willing to book a trip on a whim when cheap travel pops up, check out Scott's Cheap Flights.
- **Don't splurge on a hotel you're just going to sleep in**. If you're going sightseeing, you likely won't spend much time in your room, so it's not worth it to book the nicest hotel. Just ensure it's close to transit or can otherwise get you to all the things you want to see.
- **Experience the real culture on the cheap**. Walking around with the locals is free, so you don't need to have paid activities booked every day. Get food from local corner restaurants, which are typically cheap, authentic, and delicious. Take public transit, which is affordable and reliable in many European and Asian countries.

As an example of how to leverage these travel tips to save, here is a day I spent with a couple friends in Paris. We woke up in our hotel room above a restaurant, with just enough space to squeeze in 3 twin beds. That cost us $100 a night, so $33 each. We joined the commuters on a morning walk and fueled up for the day with fresh quiche from a local shop for $4. We paid $8 to climb up the Eiffel Tower and get some beautiful views of the city. For lunch, we grabbed a bottle of a delicious French merlot, a baguette, and some cheese and meat for a nice picnic in a park, costing $5 each. We continued to walk the city, checking out Notre-Dame and the Louvre, before settling down at a little bistro to splurge on a $14 meal that included some more local wine. The total for that day, including lodging, was $64.

Minimize other recurring expenses

It's way too easy in today's economy to accumulate a bunch of subscriptions: Amazon Prime, Spotify, Netflix, Disney Plus, a cable package, Kindle unlimited, Blue Apron, and Stitch Fix or Dollar Shave Club (depending on whether you need the latest fashion or just a good shave). Each of these seems harmless enough by itself. But if you add up the price of all those subscriptions I just mentioned, you're approaching $4,000 per year in subscriptions. Over the course of 30 years, if you had saved and invested that money instead, you'd have an extra $550,000.

The easiest way to reduce your spending here is to go from big to small; that is, look at your biggest expenditure first and determine if you can eliminate it. From my list above, Blue Apron is the most expensive, and I covered how to replace this with home-cooked meals earlier. Next is the cable package, which should be another easy one to eliminate by determining which shows you really want and finding the cheapest way to watch them via streaming services. You can also likely cut back to one streaming service without much sacrifice.

Eliminating cable and extra streaming services has tangential benefits, as well. Studies show that watching more TV leads to lower levels of happiness (according to Psychology Today). So rather than plopping down on the couch in front of the TV after work, you can do something productive like working on your side hustle or another activity that will actually improve your life satisfaction.

Alright, I'll stop lecturing now and instead give you a tip to save money and have access to multiple streaming services: split them with friends or family. If your parents have cable, you have Netflix, and your brother has Disney+, you can each get the advantages of all 3 for a fraction of the cost by sharing your login information. Technically, this is against the terms of these services, meaning they could cancel your subscription. However, this does not happen in practice, so go ahead and save some money.

Another great place to look for savings is on your cell phone bill. Personally, I love new technology. I bought an iPhone 3G when it first came out and hacked it so I could run custom apps. It's important for me to have a modern phone. And even for my needs, I only upgrade my phone every 3 years. And if you can make your phone last longer than that, you will save big. Additionally, look to buy your phone outright (not bundled with a subscription) and move to one of the budget networks that run on the same towers as Verizon or AT&T. Examples include Visible and Cricket, which are actually owned by Verizon and AT&T to provide a separate brand for price-conscious customers. Many people can cut their cell phone bills in half for the same level of service by doing this.

Ensure your partner is financially compatible

In a Bogleheads forum discussion about expenses, one poster wisely summarized that "most Americans make 3 huge financial mistakes in life which cripple their financial future:

- Too much house
- Too much car
- Wrong spouse"

If you and your partner have vastly different views on finances, it will harm not only your net worth, but also your relationship.

According to MagnifyMoney's divorce and debt survey, financial troubles are one of the leading causes of divorce, with 20% of divorces primarily attributed to financial issues. And the number is even worse for higher income couples – 33% of divorces for spouses who earn $100,000 or more.

To hit your financial and relationship goals, you need to ensure your partner is financially compatible. If you have a goal to save $40,000 per year and retire in your early 30's but your spouse's main goal is to live in an expensive house and drive nice cars, you will either need to reconsider your goals or reconsider your relationship. If instead you can share your financial goals to accumulate wealth, your journey will be much easier.

The best time to assess this is before you are married and before you have combined finances. Since I doubt you'll be talking about your 401k balances on your first date, it will likely be some time before you get a sense of your partner's financial situation. Keeping your finances separate as long as possible mitigates the risk of losing too much if the relationship doesn't work out. Some people even advocate keeping separate accounts during marriage. But even if you do this, your money accumulated during marriage will likely not be separate legally and will be split between you in the case of a divorce.

Rachel will probably be mad at me for including her in the "Expenses" section of the book, but she has been a perfect example of a financially compatible partner. Even before we met, she was living below her means and quickly paying off her student loan debt. Being on the same page about saving was key to reaching our goal of $1 million net worth by age 30.

Avoid lifestyle creep

Lifestyle creep refers to the subconscious gradual increase in spending as income rises. It is the feeling of "I've worked hard to make this money; I deserve to spend it." Common examples including flying business class instead of economy, buying luxury furniture, eating out more, and buying more expensive cars.

If you follow the advice in this book, you will increase your income. But that increase will go to waste if you succumb to lifestyle creep rather than making intentional decisions about your spending. Remember that studies show you will get accustomed to the nicer things you buy, resulting in a life that will feel the same but with lighter pockets.

As an extreme example of how lifestyle creep can cause financial trouble, let's look at Sam Dogen, aka the Financial Samurai. Sam retired at age 34 with a $3 million net worth. Between his real estate and investment portfolio, he expected to generate about $260k per year in investment income. His retirement income alone was in the top 4% of all income earners in the country, clearly enough for any reasonable retirement.

However, through extreme lifestyle creep, Sam found that income was not enough. His expenses in retirement were $310,000 per year! That spending forced him to come out of retirement, seeking to accumulate another $1.5 million before he can retire again.

There are a few clear examples of the crazy lifestyle creep that put Sam in this predicament. He insisted on buying a house in San Francisco. He needed this house to be not just in the Bay Area, where he could find an expensive but manageable home, but in San Francisco proper, where he says $310,000 will give him a middle-class life (albeit with a view of the ocean). Because he lives in the city, he does not want his kids to attend public school and will instead pay an obscene $70,000 per year to send them both to private school.

These are Sam's choices to make. However, it is hard for me to believe that spending $310,000 a year to live in San Francisco makes Sam's life better than if he paid half of that to live a few miles away in Hillsborough and was able to head into the city whenever he wanted.

Regardless of what you choose to prioritize, ensure your spending is a conscious decision rather than a case of lifestyle creep. Doing so will optimize your expenses to rapidly accumulate wealth.

This doesn't mean living a life of deprivation; rather, it empowers you to spend money on the things you truly desire.

Ultimately, the choice is yours: driving a BMW or accumulating an extra $850,000.

How I did it

Growing up in a frugal household and learning to save up my weekly allowance, I started my adult life with low expenses by habit. Because of this, I did not develop a strict budget. Instead, I made conscious decisions to buy only what I really wanted, and I bought those things as cheaply as possible. This helped me leverage my competitive nature to see if I could beat my personal records in saving year-over-year.

Because I started my career in a well-paying job in a low-cost city, it would have been easy to succumb to lifestyle creep like many of my peers. I could have lived in a fancy new apartment, bought a luxury car, and racked up $100 bar tabs every weekend. Instead, I rented a 3-bedroom house with two friends where we each paid $400 a month. In addition to maintaining low housing expenses, this arrangement also helped limit my entertainment spending, as our hobbies of beer pong, videogames, and watching The Bachelor were pretty cheap.

While a car is a necessity in central Illinois, I was able to keep my transportation costs relatively low. I saved up and used cash to buy a 4-year-old Mazda, replacing my 15-year-old Ford with rear-wheel drive and no antilock braking, improving my odds of surviving the winter. Minimizing these typically large expenses allowed me to save big early, spending only $23,000 at age 23 with a $68,000 salary. I also reserved spending for things that really improved my quality of life…and a few early-20's purchases with my roommates, such as our used ping pong table and full bar-sized Jägermeister tap.

After that low cost of living, moving to San Francisco was certainly a shock. It was painful realizing that I'd be paying almost 10 times as much in housing (also influenced by the fact that I now had a fiancée who wasn't too keen on having roommates). But other than rent and taxes, my other expenses didn't change much. As I shared before, Rachel and I sold one of our cars since we only needed one for her to commute to work while I could walk, bike, or take public transit. This saved us about $12,000 per year. My travel spending also increased a bit due to flights to see family and friends throughout the year, putting my expenses at about $54,000. However, this increase in expenses was more than offset by my increase in income, allowing me to ramp up my saving rate even more to nearly $100,000 per year.

When Rachel and I left San Francisco for Chicago, we significantly cut our housing expense while keeping our salaries level. This would have been another time lifestyle creep could have gotten the best of us. In our late 20's, many of our peers were purchasing houses much bigger than they needed and in areas they didn't expect to be long-term. We chose to keep a small, single-bedroom apartment and invest the savings.

We also didn't lose sight of the small expenses that can add up. We cut out cable and streaming, instead working out a deal to use my parents' login so Rachel could stream The Real Housewives and I could watch sports. Outside of that, I didn't have much time to watch TV anyway between my side hustles and other more active hobbies.

Rachel and I enjoy eating out, and we do a dinner date night every couple weeks. Outside of that, we keep our food spending very low. I have made it a point to always bring my lunch to work, made easier with Rachel's intense meal planning regimen, and Rachel switched to her free coffee at work rather than going to Starbucks every day. We rarely do takeout or order delivery, instead cooking up meals from the grocery store.

However, I'd be lying if I said we've been able to fully avoid lifestyle creep. We've lived in some nice apartments in premium locations, I buy a more expensive brand of protein powder, and I haven't stayed at a cheap hostel while traveling in a few years. But we've largely kept our expenses in check, meaning our saving rate has continued to increase along with our income.

Besides focusing on cost-cutting, I chose to prioritize spending in a couple areas. The first is travel. Over the past five years, I have been to Japan, Switzerland, Italy, Germany, Austria, France, Spain, England, Costa Rica, and Mexico, and dozens of cities here in the U.S. Fortunately, this travel was largely subsidized through credit card rewards, as I kept a lookout for big signup bonuses and charged work travel to my personal cards whenever possible.

I also prioritized spending on housing that gave me a short commute. I've never commuted more than 25 minutes and have been able to walk to work for the past 4 years. This has given me more time and energy to use during my day job while also working on my side hustles. Plus, a 25-minute walk is a great way to reset after a long day at the office.

While the number one key to hitting my million-dollar milestone was quickly increasing income, it wouldn't have been possible without keeping my expenses moderate, focusing my spending on the areas I valued most. If you can make your spending an exercise in intentional prioritization, you will see similar success and start to quickly build your assets. Next, we'll cover how you can protect those assets.

CHAPTER 5

Protect your assets

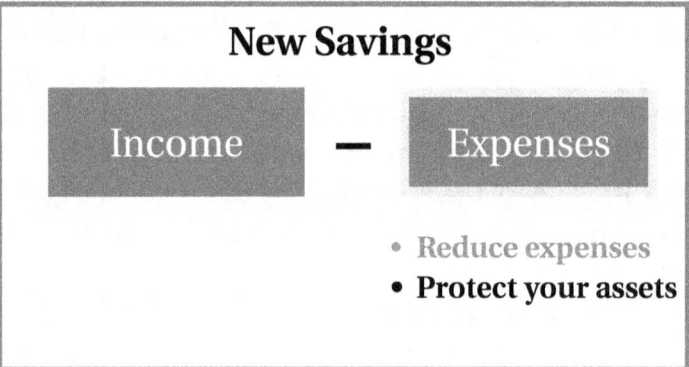

I'll be honest: protecting your assets is not very exciting. If investing is the George Clooney of personal finance, then health and insurance are the Jonah Hill and Seth Rogan. They're not sexy, but they are key players in your financial story. Without them, it is impossible to optimize your net worth equation. To make this as painless as possible, I'll give you only what you need to know: protect your health and your wealth.

Protect your health – your human capital

If you are just starting on the path to significant wealth accumulation, you may not have much to show in terms of assets. That's fine, because right now your biggest asset is your human capital: your ability to earn money going forward. That ability is significantly hampered if your health goes south, so your health is critical to your financial success.

The best thing you can do for your health is to exercise on a regular basis. Many people, especially those working hard in their day jobs and side hustles, believe they're too busy and don't have time. However, taking 30 minutes to an hour to exercise will boost your productivity enough to more than make up for the time spent at the gym. A study from Briston University found that working out results in a 20% increase in ability to finish work on time and a 40% increase in motivation to work. This means that in addition to the health benefits, taking the time to exercise has a net positive impact on your productivity. If you're having trouble getting into the habit of exercising, consider it as one of your job responsibilities. You need it if you want to perform optimally in your day job, and you *really* need it if you want to have the energy to be productive in your side hustle.

So far, I've only highlighted the financial benefits of exercising. It also reduces your risk of cardiovascular disease and cancer, improves your long-term mental health, and increases your chances of living longer. I'm not a doctor, but those all sound like good things to me.

Another aspect of your health that is important to your financial success is sleep. Like exercise, many driven people have trouble finding the time to get an adequate night of sleep. However, lack of sufficient sleep has many negative consequences.

First, lack of sleep leads to reduced focus and motivation, irritability, and bad decision making, all poor traits for those seeking career success. Studies have shown that sleep deprivation costs the average person 11 days of productivity each year. So if you earn $100,000 a year, it's costing you $5,000. That $5,000 per year, compounded for investment returns over 30 years, is $680,0000.

So how much sleep is "adequate?" The American Academy of Sleep Medicine recommends between 7-8 hours a night. Working professionals average an hour under that, around 6.5 hours a night, and anecdotally, I know many people with side hustles who get much less than that. These people are shooting themselves in the foot by skimping on sleep.

Like exercise, sleep is important for your long-term health and to protect your human capital. To be financially successful, you must become an expert at prioritizing your time. Once you do that, it should not be too hard to budget 8 hours a day for sleep and exercise.

Beyond sleep and exercise, you should also look to leverage your more traditional healthcare benefits, many of which are free. All health insurance plans, even high deductible plans, will typically cover preventative care at 100%, meaning no cost to you. This includes an annual check-up with the doctor, blood work to monitor things like your cholesterol and glucose levels, vaccines, and a dentist appointment twice a year.

Insurance companies pay these expenses in full for a reason, and it's not because they're nice. Preventative care saves them money by reducing potential future health issues. This is also a good thing for you, as it reduces the amount you will need to pay out-of-pocket for larger medical expenses and protects your human capital, your ability to earn money in the future.

Let's look at vaccines, for example. According to the Centers for Disease Control and Prevention, the influenza vaccine is typically around 40-50% effective. That means by taking the 15 minutes to get a free flu shot at your local pharmacy, you are now about half as likely to get the flu this year. Assuming the average flu would sideline you for one workweek, that means the flu shot gives you an extra 2.5 productive days per year. If you make $100,000 a year, those 2.5 days are worth $1,000. That's a solid tradeoff for 15 minutes and a prick in the shoulder.

Finally, it's also important to take care of your mental health and not be afraid to cut back on work when needed. When striving to reach an ambitious goal like becoming a millionaire, it is easy to become fully absorbed and neglect other aspects of your life.

This will inevitably lead to burnout, even for those with the highest work ethic. Here are a few tips to help keep your balance.

Find a hobby that is completely for fun, not at all related to making money. This is important so you have something you can do to relax your mind for a bit. For example, I enjoy riding my Vespa around town, watching sports, and playing online videogames with my brothers.

Keep a strong social group. While you're busy pursuing your goals, it's easy to put everything else in life on the backburner, including your social network. And I'm not talking about your Facebook friends and Instagram followers; I'm talking about your real-life friends and family.

The research paper "if money doesn't make you happy then you probably aren't spending it right" outlines that spending money on friends or to see friends increases overall happiness. So don't hesitate to spend time and give up a little money to keep connected with them – whether that just means grabbing drinks or a meal, or buying a plane ticket to see the people you love. This has been really important for me when going through stressful times at a new job. I knew that even if I needed to make drastic career changes, my life wouldn't be completely turned upside down thanks to my wife, family, and friends.

Don't hesitate to see a mental health professional. Just as you see a doctor to address physical health issues, you should see a doctor for mental health issues. Fortunately, you won't have to spend a fortune to do so. The mental health parity law passed in 2008 requires insurance companies to treat mental and behavioral health coverage equal to or better than physical health coverage. That means insurers can't charge a $20 copay for a routine doctor's visit but say you're on the hook for the full bill at a psychologist. Just like with your physical health, don't wait until it's an emergency to get a check-up. There is no shame in doing the responsible thing by seeing a mental health doctor. If you don't know where to look for mental health services, Mental Health America can point you in the right direction.

Taking action to stay healthy is good for your finances and good for your life. If you can allocate time to exercise and sleep, make the most of your free medical benefits, and take your mental health seriously, you'll be setting yourself up for financial success.

Protect your wealth with insurance

Let's imagine you've followed every piece of advice so far in this book. It's now 10 years later, and you just crossed $1 million in net worth. Congratulations! To celebrate, you're going out to a not-too-fancy restaurant with your buddies. You're cruising in city traffic on the way there when suddenly the big SUV in front of you swerves into the left lane, revealing 2 pedestrians standing in the middle of your lane. You slam on the brakes but can't stop in time, and you hit them at 20 mph. They are rushed to the hospital to receive extensive treatment, and you're deemed liable for $1,200,000 in the pedestrians' medical bills and lost wages. Your state-minimum liability insurance pays out its limit of $50,000. You are now on the hook for the remaining $1,150,000. You just went from being a millionaire to having a net worth of -$150,000 and garnished wages for the next few years, all from a random incident one night.

You probably don't like thinking about these scenarios; nobody does. Fortunately, there is a way to limit your risk of financial ruin from situations like this: insurance. At its most basic level, buying insurance is trading a known amount of money each year to eliminate the small chance of facing financial hardship from an accident. Think of it as the opposite of a lottery ticket. When you buy a lottery ticket (which is hopefully very rarely), you pay a small amount of money for the potential of winning a big, life-changing amount of money. When you buy insurance, you pay a small amount of money to ensure you don't *lose* a big, life-changing amount of money.

I know insurance is likely near the bottom of the list of things you'd like to learn about. Luckily, I've done the research for you and will provide an overview of the various types of insurance you should be aware of. I'll also share some tips to keep the costs reasonable from an insurance industry insider.

You can optimize your insurance expenditure by purchasing it only to protect against losing a life-changing amount of money. Because people are naturally risk averse, the pain of losing $5 outweighs the joy of gaining $5. To mitigate that pain, people buy extended warranties on cars, phones, computers, and more. Those purchases are bad financial decisions, and it doesn't require any fancy math to prove it. As mentioned earlier, insurance companies are not inherently nice. If the insurer didn't earn a profit by paying out less money than it collected, the company wouldn't offer the product.

That means you as a consumer of insurance are losing money on average. But that's fine, as the reason to buy insurance is not to come out ahead. Instead, it is to mitigate or eliminate the risk of an event that could be financially devastating. Your $500 TV broke? That's not financially devastating – either buy a new one or go without TV if you can't afford it. Your $400,000 house burned down? That's financially devastating and worth insuring.

With those principles as a foundation, I'll now give the world's fastest overview of the types of insurance you might need in priority order:

- **Health insurance**: choose your plan based on premium and out-of-pocket max
    - If you don't expect to go to the doctor much, minimize premium
    - If you expect to go to the doctor a lot, minimize out-of-pocket max
    - Look for a High Deductible Health Plan with an HSA to provide a tax-free investment vehicle

- **Disability (income) insurance**: buy long-term disability to cover your baseline expenses
- **Auto and homeowners**: select liability limits to cover your net worth and buy as little property coverage as you can financially tolerate
- **Life**: you only need it if you have financial dependents. If so, buy term life to cover dependent's expenses.

If that insurance jargon doesn't make sense to you or you want more detail, see the world's second-fastest overview of insurance below.

Health insurance

When determining what health insurance plan is best for you, there are two main financial aspects to consider: premium and out-of-pocket maximum. The premium you pay is your guaranteed minimum expense. In a best-case scenario where you're completely healthy and only get free preventative care like an annual check-up, your premium will be your total cost for medical care. On the flip side, your out-of-pocket maximum is your worst-case scenario. If you were in a bad accident and needed hundreds of thousands of dollars' worth of medical care, you would hit your out-of-pocket max, and your total medical cost for the year would be your premium plus your out-of-pocket maximum.

Thus, your premium and out-of-pocket max define the ends of the medical expense spectrum, and you'll likely fall somewhere in between. Deductibles and copays also matter, but they will still put your total medical expenditure somewhere in this range. You can use these numbers to estimate your medical costs next year across plans and choose the one that you expect will cost the least overall. If you're healthy and don't expect to go to the doctor much, shoot for a low premium, which is what I typically do. If you have a pre-existing condition or expect to go to the doctor often (for example, if you're trying to get pregnant), focus more on keeping your out-of-pocket max low, since you're likely to hit it.

Either way, assuming you're accumulating some money in your investment portfolio, you should be able to go with higher deductibles since minor medical expenses won't be a financial risk to you. In this case, you can consider a High Deductible Health Plan (HDHP), which enables you to contribute to a Health Savings Account (HSA).

HSAs are commonly confused with Flexible Spending Accounts (FSAs). Both allow you to avoid paying income tax on money you use for medical expenses. However, FSA balances only last for one year, while HSAs can be used as a true saving and investment vehicle. Be sure to read your plan documentation so you know which one you're getting. If you have an FSA, it's worthwhile to fund it up to your near-certain medical expenses for the year. This will save the equivalent of your marginal tax rate (typically 30-40%) on these expenses. However, be careful not to overcontribute, since FSAs are use-it-or-lose-it every year.

If you have a high deductible plan with an HSA, you essentially have another tax-advantaged investment vehicle available to you. In fact, HSAs are the best possible investment account. They function like a 401k in that you can put money in pre-tax (except in a couple states). But they are even better than 401ks because money you withdraw from an HSA to cover medical expenses is completely tax free, including things your health insurance doesn't cover, like dental and vision. This makes the HSA the only investment vehicle which enables you to never pay tax – not at contribution and not at withdrawal.

Withdrawals can be made at any time to cover prior medical expenses (no matter how long ago the expense was incurred), so a common strategy is to pay medical expenses out of normal cash flow while letting the HSA investment portfolio grow over the course of many years. By doing this and keeping your receipts, you can wait decades to withdraw from your now much larger account for free. For example, if you pay $2,000 per year in out-of-pocket medical expenses for 30 years, you can then withdraw a tax-free lump sum of $60,000. For more detail on this strategy, see the Bogleheads HSA wiki page.

Another medical savings tip that is especially helpful if you have an HSA is to consider paying for prescriptions out of pocket rather than through insurance. When considering co-pays and deductibles, I found I could buy my recurring prescription for 25% of the cost at GoodRx, a pharmacy coupon site. If you have prescriptions, take a look and don't assume you get the best deal through your insurance.

Disability (income) insurance

Disability insurance is more aptly called income insurance. It replaces a portion of your income if you are unable to work due to injury or illness and is the most under-purchased insurance for the American workforce. When you're in the accumulation phase of gaining net worth before retirement, your most valuable asset is your human capital—so you should insure your most valuable asset.

Disability insurance is sold as either short-term or long-term. Short-term disability will typically cover a period up to 6 months and is often fully or partially paid by your employer. If it's not, whether you should purchase depends on your emergency fund and investment portfolio. For example, since I can cover 6 months' expenses from my portfolio, I don't have short-term disability insurance. This saves me from a hefty monthly premium payment.

Long-term disability is the more important coverage, kicking in when you can't work for more than 6 months, typically going all the way to retirement age. This is critical to have because it will protect you in case your health prevents you from earning money in the long run. Generally, this will be offered at a range around 50-60% of your salary, and you'll want to ensure you can at least cover your necessary expenses with your coverage selection.

Auto and homeowners/renters insurance

When considering auto and home insurance, you mainly think about the stuff you're insuring: your car and your house. But the liability component is actually more important because that's what can cause you true financial hardship. Theoretically, you could be sued and held liable for any amount, up to millions for a severe enough injury. However, a general rule of thumb is to buy liability limits of at least $300,000 and increase your limits as your net worth rises.

Following this strategy, as your net worth grows to $500,000 and more, you likely won't be able to buy high enough liability insurance directly on your auto and homeowners policies. This is where umbrella insurance comes in. As the name suggests, umbrella insurance offers an additional layer of security above your auto and home policies. In the pedestrian accident example, umbrella insurance would cover your liability above your auto policy limits, leaving your net worth intact.

With your liability covered, how much insurance should you buy to protect your actual property, your car and house? As little as you can tolerate. Financial losses on these tangible items are limited to the value of the item. Once you build up your net worth, you can save over 50% on property insurance by increasing your deductibles and removing comprehensive and collision (full coverage) on your car. When you have a $200,000 investment portfolio, you don't need to pay an insurance company money to avoid the small chance of a $8,000 loss when your car gets totaled or your roof gets damaged in a storm.

As a final tip in the auto and home insurance space, be sure to shop around for insurance every couple years. The pricing algorithms for these products are incredibly complex, and you could get very different prices from two companies for no apparent reason. To use this to your advantage, shop around on different companies' websites to see how much you could save by switching.

Life insurance

I chose to cover life insurance last for a reason. In the insurance industry, people describe life insurance as the "insurance that isn't bought but is sold." In other words, many people are sold policies they don't need. The purpose of life insurance is to help people who are financially dependent on you and would face financial hardship from your death. Until you have someone financially dependent on you (spouse or kids), you should not buy life insurance.

If you have dependents and need life insurance, you should only buy term life, not whole life or universal life insurance. Whole and universal life mix an investment vehicle with insurance when there is no reason to do so. Well, there is a reason for the salesperson: to obscure the line between insurance premium and investment so you don't realize the insane commission you're paying. It's typical for the salesperson to take 50-100% of your first year's premium as commission.

Instead of buying whole or universal life, look to buy guaranteed renewable term life for the amount of time you need it, with a bit of extra padding. "Guaranteed renewable" means that regardless of how your health changes during that time period, you will still be able to purchase coverage. The amount of life insurance to purchase is a bit tricky. As a rule of thumb, determine roughly how much money you will need to support those dependent on your income, and multiply by the number of years it is needed. For example, if your household averages $60,000 in annual expenses and your kids will be independent in 18 years, your starting point would be $1,080,000.

You can effectively protect your wealth by insuring things that would be a real financial hardship, like disability, and avoiding insurance for stuff you can cover on your own. Combine that with protecting your health, and your most important assets will be safe. With that covered, we'll move on to how you can make your money work for you through investing.

SECTION III

Make your money work for you

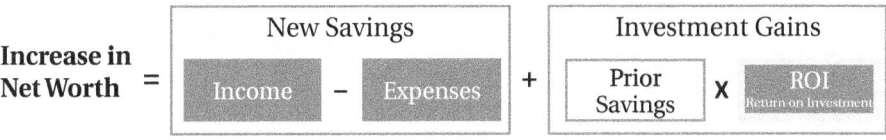

We've now covered how to optimize two of the three components you control in the net worth equation. You know how to maximize your earnings and reduce expenses to generate substantial annual savings. Now, it's time to put that money to work by optimizing the final component: your investment returns.

CHAPTER 6

Set your investment strategy

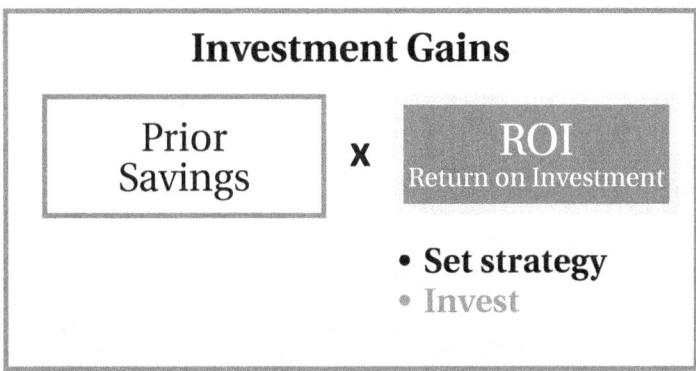

By investing wisely, you will convert your hard-earned savings into financial freedom, enabling a life where you never again need to work for money.

Since investing is such a prominent topic in personal finance, you may be wondering why I waited until this point in the book to cover it. There are two reasons.

Reason #1: Investing doesn't matter until you save.
Increasing your investment rate of return cannot make an impact until you actually have substantial money to invest. If you want to grow net worth quickly, you will need to rely on significant savings by increasing income and reducing expenses.

For example, let's consider Isaac, a knowledgeable investor who can consistently earn a return on investment (ROI) around 10% while saving $15,000 annually. This is close to the long-term return of the U.S. stock market. Susan, on the other hand, doesn't have a knack for investment and only earns 5% annually. However, she is a disciplined budgeter and saves $30,000 a year. In essence, Isaac is twice as good at investing, while Susan is twice as good at saving. Let's see how these two compare as they're getting started in their careers.

Year	Net Worth	
	Isaac	Susan
1	$ 15,000	$ 30,000
3	$ 49,650	$ 94,575
5	$ 91,577	$ 165,769

By year 5, Susan has accumulated a net worth of $165,000, while Isaac is almost $75,000 behind. His superior investments have little effect because of his small starting portfolio and the short timeframe.

Reason #2: Investing is easy.

Despite what the financial services industry wants you to think, developing and executing on your investment strategy is easy. This is the simplest component of wealth accumulation, and it is surely easier than what you do in your day job. In fact, you could have your investment portfolio 90% optimized by following this one-sentence piece of advice:

Buy target date funds in your retirement accounts and watch them grow.

It really is that simple. If you have money sitting in a checking or savings account because you don't think you know enough about investing, you can put this book down now and invest in a target date fund (for example Vanguard's Target Retirement 2055).

But if you'd like the remaining 10% optimization (or you have no idea what target date funds and retirement accounts are), these next two chapters will provide all the knowledge you need to set and execute an investment strategy to become a millionaire, *without* a financial advisor. We'll cover how to attain this final 10% by optimizing your asset allocation, reducing your investment expenses, and leveraging some little-known techniques to minimize your taxes.

Despite investing being relatively simple and dependent on saving, I do not want to undermine its importance in maintaining and growing your accumulated wealth to support a long and fruitful period of financial freedom. To illustrate, let's check in on Isaac and Susan a bit later in their careers, assuming the same saving rates and ROI as before.

Year	Net Worth Isaac	Susan
1	$ 15,000	$ 30,000
3	$ 49,650	$ 94,575
5	$ 91,577	$ 165,769
10	$ 239,061	$ 377,337
15	$ 476,587	$ 647,357
20	$ 859,125	$ 991,979
25	$ 1,475,206	$ 1,431,813
30	$ 2,467,410	$ 1,993,165

Over a 25 or 30-year timeframe, Isaac's superior investments give him a higher net worth even though he saves only half as much each year. As Isaac continues to accumulate more wealth and earn a 10% return on that wealth each year, his annual investment returns rapidly surpass his saving rate. By year 25, he is accumulating $150k a year in investments alone.

This is the magic of compound returns: you earn returns on both your initial investment and the returns already earned in the past. To illustrate, the table below shows a starting investment of $1,000 with 10% returns each year over the course of 7 years.

Year	Investment Return	Portfolio Value
0	-	$1,000
1	$100	$1,100
2	$110	$1,210
3	$121	$1,331
4	$133	$1,464
5	$146	$1,611
6	$161	$1,772
7	$177	$1,949

In year 1, our investment return is $100, or 10% of the initial investment. This gives us a total of $1,100 invested. In year 2, we also get a 10% return, but that return is calculated based on the $1,100 amount, giving us $110 in gains and bringing the total value to $1,210. Repeating this over 7 years, the ending balance is $1,949, almost double the initial investment, representing a total return of 95% (much greater than the 70% return earned without compounding). This also illustrates the previously mentioned rule of 72. In this example, 72 divided by our 10% rate of return equals 7.2 years to double.

When discussing returns throughout this book, I typically speak in terms of real returns. Real returns reflect your increase in purchasing power after accounting for inflation. For example, let's say your investments grew 9% in a year but all your expenses increased 2% due to inflation. Even though your nominal returns were 9%, you can't afford 9% more than you could the year prior. The difference between your nominal returns and inflation is your real return, in this case 7%.

Clearly, investing is an important part of becoming (and staying) a millionaire. With that foundation set, let's dive into the most important investment decisions you will need to make, in priority order.

Set your desired asset allocation

I mentioned earlier that you could do very well in investing by following a one-sentence piece of advice:

Buy target date funds in your retirement accounts and watch them grow.

This works in part because target date funds automatically follow an appropriate asset allocation. Asset allocation is how your investment portfolio is spread across the different classes of possible investments. Investments that tend to have higher average returns over the long term also have more volatility in their value over the short term. In other words, you need to take greater risk to see greater returns. If you are planning to retire in 25 years, you can afford to see the value of your investments go up and down in the short term. If you are going to retire next year, you don't want to risk a random downswing hurting your ability to retire.

Target date funds automatically transition your investments from high earning, highly volatile accounts to low earning, stable accounts as they progress towards the selected retirement year. That automatic transition is helpful, but it comes at the expense of slightly higher fees. If you want to be more hands-on and minimize your fees (thus maximizing returns), you'll need to set your own asset allocation using the three primary asset classes.

- **Stocks** (equities) represent partial ownership of a corporation and earn returns through increasing prices as well as paying cash dividends to shareholders. Equities have the highest short-term volatility of the three main asset classes; it is possible for equities to lose or gain 50% or more over the course of a year. In return for this risk, equities offer the highest average returns, especially over a long timeframe.

- **Bonds** (fixed income) represent debt, typically issued by a corporation or government entity. With bonds, you are essentially loaning cash to a firm that will provide periodic interest payments. Investment grade bonds have a very low risk of default, so the value of bonds is generally more stable than that of stocks, but the average returns are lower.
- **Cash and cash equivalents** cover any funds in a money market fund, savings account, checking account, or even dollar bills stashed under your mattress. Cash equivalents have the least risk of the three asset classes and thus the lowest returns. Any funds you hold in cash will likely lose purchasing power over time due to inflation.

To set your allocation across these asset classes, there are two predominant considerations: investment horizon and risk tolerance. Investment horizon is the length of time the money will be invested before you expect to need it to make purchases. For short horizons, you want your funds invested in a way to minimize fluctuations in value. Take fixed expenses, such as rent or mortgage payments as an example. Let's say you set aside $1,500 from your paycheck each month to pay your mortgage. It would be foolish to invest this money in the stock market without backup cash available. If the stock market declined in the month, a very common occurrence, you wouldn't be able to pay your mortgage.

On the flip side, for long horizons, you want most of your funds in the higher-risk, higher-reward class of equities. While the value of equites can drop in the short-term, these fluctuations do not matter for a long-term investor. Because you don't need to spend the money immediately, you can safely ride out market turbulence, allowing your portfolio's value to grow exponentially until you reach retirement. And you can rest assured that it will grow. While we cannot predict the future with 100% certainty, we can get a useful approximation by looking at outcomes from the past. Here is how the U.S. stock market has grown over the last 150 years.

As you can see, the value of stocks has grown substantially and rather consistently over time. $1 invested in the U.S. stock market in 1871 would be worth $460,000 in July of 2020. This long-term growth completely overshadows any short-term dips, making even the Great Depression and COVID-19 blips on the radar.

While the stock market is "risky" in the sense that its value can drop in a day, it is not risky for long time horizons. Over the history of the stock market, every single 30-year period has seen real (inflation adjusted) annual returns of over 5%. This resilient growth over the course of 150 years means we can be confident the upward trend will continue in the future. Investors with a long horizon should have an equity-heavy portfolio to take advantage of this growth.

Between these two ends of the investment horizon spectrum, a blend of asset classes makes sense. For example, a 50-year-old looking to retire in 5 years and start withdrawing from their portfolio would want the risk of equities balanced out with the reliability of bonds and perhaps some cash to ensure the portfolio does not dip too low to cover expenses.

A good rule-of-thumb for asset allocation based on horizon can be obtained by looking at the glide path of Vanguard's target retirement funds. These funds are created with a target retirement year, which is the investment horizon when saving for retirement. As an investor ages and gets closer to retirement, the horizon becomes shorter, and the asset allocation shifts.

Inv. Horizon (Years)	Stocks	Bonds
25+	90%	10%
20	83%	17%
15	76%	24%
10	69%	31%
5	61%	39%
0	51%	49%

The above chart provides a good starting point, but the other aspect to consider when setting your asset allocation is your personal risk tolerance – from both a financial and psychological consideration. On the financial side, what is the risk you face from your portfolio losing value? Will you need to work another year or two before retirement? Or will you be unable to put food on the table? For most people reading this book, it is the former, which justifies taking more risk in return for higher expected returns.

On the psychological side, you must choose an asset allocation that prevents you from losing sleep at night or sabotaging your own returns by selling early. As mentioned in the "Protect Your Assets" chapter, your greatest asset early in your career is your human capital. Investing in a way that causes undue stress is bad for your long-term physical and financial health. A good rule of thumb is to assume that equities can drop 50% in a year. So if you can only stomach a 30% portfolio loss without panic-selling your equity allocation, you should have at most 60% of your portfolio in equities.

You must be realistic about your tolerance for market downswings and ability to weather them without making irrational changes (or letting them keep you up at night). However, I hope that after reading this book you recognize that it's pointless to stress over short-term fluctuations and you can become comfortable with a more aggressive asset allocation. It is much easier to stomach short-term losses when you realize that the market will be up in the long run. If you can stay strong through the first few dips, you will be set. Trust me, the guy who lost $35,000 betting on a Norfolk State basketball game, it gets easier as you go. You'll get to a point where you chuckle when the media freaks out about the next big crash and see it as an opportunity to buy at a discount. That was my mindset even *after* I saw my net worth drop over $75,000 in one day due to the 2020 coronavirus pandemic.

An allocation of mostly equities is simply the fastest way to accumulate wealth and achieve financial independence. Additionally, it is actually *less risky* over a long timeframe because the higher expected returns reduce the risk you'll run out of money. This is why I am currently invested in 100% equities and plan to keep it that way for some time.

One final distinction that is often made with regard to asset allocation is the percentage of equities that are domestic (U.S.-based) vs. international. This is a widely debated topic in investing circles. Hardcore advocates of the efficient market hypothesis argue for portfolios that proportionally represent the market value of corporations across the total world economy. They rightfully note that successfully picking specific stocks is nearly impossible, so why would picking specific countries be any different? This contingent holds a domestic/international equity split right around 50/50 to reflect to total market value of the U.S. vs. the rest of the world.

On the other end of the spectrum, some (including the legendary Jack Bogle, founder of Vanguard) believe that owning international stocks is unnecessary. They argue that the additional costs, currency risk, and country risk involved in international investing are not worth it. Additionally, investing in the total U.S. market comes with inherent international exposure since many U.S. companies do substantial business overseas. This group holds a domestic/international equity split of close to 100/0, meaning all of their stock is U.S.-based.

So how should you choose between these two positions? My recommendation is to go somewhere in the middle. Historical performance over multi-decade periods has shown that including some international equities in your portfolio has either increased return, decreased volatility, or both. A domestic/international split of 70/30 has effectively balanced these two benefits. That seems to be the sweet spot, but anywhere between 50/50 and 100/0 is reasonable.

Adding a 70/30 domestic/international split to our baseline table for asset allocation, we end up with:

Inv. Horizon (Years)	U.S. Stocks	Intl. Stocks	Bonds
25+	63%	27%	10%
20	58%	25%	17%
15	53%	23%	24%
10	48%	21%	31%
5	43%	18%	39%
0	36%	15%	49%

This sums up all you need to know about asset allocation. You might be wondering why we haven't talked about other types of investments like real estate or small businesses. The reason is simple: this chapter is about making your money work for you, not working for your money. Over hundreds of years, stocks and bonds have proven to be a reliable, passive method of earning a solid return on your portfolio that well-outpaces inflation.

Of course, there are alternative investments available, but they either require more work from you, turning investing into a second job, or they do not have the reliable long-term returns of stocks and bonds.

- **Real estate** investing can be either passive or active. On the passive side, investors can purchase Real Estate Investment Trusts (REITs) to invest in real estate without a large capital requirement. In fact, REITs are included in most total stock market index funds. However, holding a higher allocation of REITs than the market has resulted in lower returns without much diversification benefit in the long run. On the active side, investors can purchase their own property and generate income from either renting or flipping the property. While there is certainly money to be made, it is only worth doing if you're seeking an extra job as a landlord or house renovator.
- **Small businesses** can be excellent investments for those who can blend their skillset and passion with a real market opportunity. That is why, as discussed earlier, millionaires are disproportionately small business owners. However, this is more of a career choice than an investment. For example, moderately wealthy people commonly purchase franchises to generate income from their accumulated wealth, only to find themselves working longer hours than ever and facing greater risk of losing everything. There is a common saying that "buying a franchise is buying a job."
- **Gold,** unlike real estate and small businesses, is a truly passive investment. Proponents typically buy either physical 1 oz. bullion coins or invest in gold Exchange Traded Funds (ETFs) that give investors exposure to gold without physical ownership. While gold does offer some diversification benefit, its returns have not been high enough to justify holding it. Over the past century-plus, gold has an annual real return (adjusted for inflation) of 1%. Over the same time span, the return of equities is about 7%, and U.S. bonds are just under 2%. Gold is also tax-inefficient, with gains taxed at a rate of 28%, while gains from stocks and bonds are most often taxed at 15%.

- **Peer-to-peer (P2P) lending, cryptocurrency, and other recent "trends"** simply have not been proven to have the consistent long-term returns of a stock-and-bond portfolio. P2P lending is complex, tax inefficient, and requires a high number of notes to be held (700-800) for effective diversification. Cryptocurrency was widely talked about in 2017-2018 as a way to get rich quick. While some took the gamble and won, many others lost close to their entire investment. In December 2017, the price of Bitcoin fell from $20,089 to $11,833 in less than a week. Bitcoin lost 41% in a single week, 26% in a single day, and over 10% in a single hour. If you want to gamble in the latest fads for fun, that's fine, but don't call it investing and don't spend a significant amount of time or money.

Put your money in the right spot

With your asset allocation set, the next decision you need to make is where to invest your money. I don't mean specific funds just yet, but rather which of the many available investment accounts you should use. The reason this is so important is taxation. Depending on your income levels and the tax-advantaged investment vehicles you leverage, you could be taxed anywhere from 0% to 24% on your investment gains. Clearly your tax efficiency will have a significant impact on your net worth growth.

While taxation is the most complicated aspect of investing, there is a standard order of operations you can follow when determining where to invest. This order is near-optimal for the vast majority of investors.

Priority	Account	Amount
1	Emergency fund	3-12 months' expenses
2	Work 401k, 403b, or 457b	Enough to maximize company match
3	Roth IRA	Up to the limit ($6,000 in 2020)
4	Remaining tax-advantaged space	Up to the limit (depends on available accounts)
5	Early repayment of medium-interest debt	Any debt with moderately high interest rate
6	Regular taxable investment account	Any additional saving

Let's look at each of these in more detail.

1. Emergency fund and other financial emergencies

Before you start investing for longer-term goals, the first place to put your money is in an emergency fund, a stash of cash used for unexpected expenses. The most common financial emergency you need to cover is job loss, as has recently been made clear following coronavirus-related layoffs. But this fund can also cover medical bills, car breakdowns, home repairs, and other unanticipated events.

In general, it is recommended that your emergency fund cover between 3 to 12 months of expenses, depending on your income stability. A dual-income household with stable jobs can feel safe holding 3 months' worth, while a single earner with an uncertain employment status will want closer to a year's worth.

You want to hold your emergency fund in a vehicle that is low risk and highly liquid, meaning you can turn it into spendable cash quickly. Savings accounts, money market funds, and checking accounts are all good places. As you start to invest more and build significant balances in regular taxable accounts (not retirement accounts), you can reduce your emergency fund, knowing you can always sell some stocks or bonds if needed. See my Bogleheads forum post "If you have a sizable portfolio, you don't need an emergency fund" for details on why this is optimal. I currently only hold 2 months' expenses in a checking account and invest everything else according to my selected asset allocation. Even if the market dropped an unprecedented 80%, I could cover over a year's expenses, so this strategy allows me to maximize my expected return with little downside risk.

In addition to establishing an emergency fund, you want to take care of any existing financial emergencies before putting money in retirement accounts. This includes paying off any credit card debt, which is absolutely a financial emergency, with average interest rates around 20%. That is a guaranteed 20% return on your investment you won't find anywhere else.

2. Work-based retirement plan up to the company match – 401k or 403b or 457b

Once you have potential emergencies covered, your next investing priority is to take advantage of any free money offered through your work-based retirement plan, if you have one. The 401k is the standard defined-contribution retirement savings plan provided by employers. This type of plan is much more popular now than defined-benefit plans (aka pensions) because the responsibility to invest the funds falls on employees rather than the employer. This trend away from pensions will likely continue as more companies (such as GE) and government bodies (such as the state of Illinois) suffer from underfunded pensions.

403b plans, available at public schools and certain non-profits, and 457b plans, available at certain government or tax-exempt organizations, are very similar to the 401k. The advice here applies to all 3 work-based plans.

The main draw of contributing to a 401k is that you can deduct your contributions from your taxable income and instead pay taxes when you withdraw the money in retirement. For example, if your income is $100,000 and you contribute the 2020 maximum of $19,500, you are only taxed as if you earned $80,500 in income. The downside to a 401k is that you typically must wait to access the funds until age 59 ½. However, you shouldn't worry about contributing too much and being unable to access this money, as there are ways around that rule for early retirees.

A common feature of work-based plans is the employer matching a portion of your contributions. This is free money, which is why it is the first place you should invest after taking care of emergencies. Often, this match is expressed as X% match of your contributions up to Y% of your salary. For example, a company's 401k plan might match 75% of employee contributions up to 8% of salary. Thus, an employee making $100,000 can get a free $6,000 in the form of an employer match every year.

Another common feature of these plans is the choice between pre-tax or Roth contributions. Unlike traditional pre-tax 401k contributions, Roth contributions cannot be deducted from your taxable income. Instead, you pay income taxes as usual now, but when you withdraw the money in retirement, you do not pay any taxes on your capital gains. The choice between pre-tax and Roth boils down to your income tax rate today vs. what it will be when you withdraw funds in retirement. If you expect your tax rate in retirement to be lower (which is often the case due to decreased income), you should contribute pre-tax. If you have a lower-income year, meaning your tax rate will likely be higher in retirement, you should make Roth contributions. If you're not sure, you can't go wrong with saving on taxes today and choosing traditional pre-tax, especially if you're following the advice of earlier chapters and have a high income.

One last point on 401k plans: if you have any self-employment income at all, it's likely worthwhile to open a Solo 401k plan. This includes even small amounts of part-time income such as driving for Uber or doing consulting work. Being self-employed means you can contribute as both employer and employee to your 401k. The exact mechanics of this are beyond the scope of this book, but you can check out the Solo 401k page on the Bogleheads wiki for details.

3. Roth IRA up to the limit

IRA stands for Individual Retirement Account and is a personal account available to anyone working in the U.S., regardless of employer. You can sign up for a Roth IRA through a brokerage such as Fidelity, Vanguard, or Schwab. Like the Roth 401k, Roth IRA contributions are not tax-deductible today but instead grow over time tax-free. Contributing to a Roth IRA after taking advantage of any company match is often preferred to filling your entire 401k, because of better fund selection with lower expenses in a personal account. However, if your work-based plan offers good, low-cost options, it likely makes sense to fill that space up to the limit first.

Technically, only those with income below a certain threshold can contribute directly to a Roth IRA. In 2020, those limits are modified adjusted gross income below $196,000 if married filing joint or $124,000 if filing single. However, there is a simple workaround available to everyone called a "backdoor Roth IRA." To leverage a backdoor Roth, you contribute to a traditional IRA account but do not deduct the contribution from your income, making it an after-tax contribution. Then, you immediately convert the funds in the traditional IRA to a Roth IRA. Using this method, which has been legitimized by the IRS, anyone can contribute to a backdoor Roth up to the limit, which is $6,000 in 2020.

Traditional (pre-tax) IRAs are also available below a certain income threshold but are generally not recommended, as they can block future backdoor Roth contributions as your income increases.

4. Remaining tax-advantaged space – HSA, 401k, 403b, 457b, mega backdoor Roth

Priority number 2 was to contribute just enough to your work-based retirement plan to maximize your employer match. It's now time to fill in the rest of your tax-advantaged space. As mentioned earlier, you really cannot put too much money here, as there are ways to withdraw early if needed.

The first account to fill in this category is an HSA, or Health Savings Account, if you have one. The HSA is the top dog in this category because like 401k contributions, your contributions are tax-deductible today, but the bonus is that withdrawals are also tax-free when used for medical expenses. Unfortunately, most people do not have an HSA available to them. You can only contribute to an HSA if you have a High Deductible Health Plan (HDHP), either through your employer or privately purchased. And as we covered earlier, an HDHP might not be the best choice if you have near-certain medical expenses coming in the next year.

If you do have an HSA, the optimal way to use it is like any other retirement vehicle – let it continue to compound while you pay medical expenses, like deductibles, out-of-pocket. If you keep your receipts, you can wait until retirement, when your balance will be much larger, to withdraw and reimburse yourself for those old expenses. Alternatively, you can choose to use your HSA like most people and withdraw for medical expenses along the way. While not optimal from an investment return standpoint, it's much better than not using an HSA at all and requires a bit less organization.

The next-best place to invest is your work-based plan (401k, 403b, or 457b) up to the IRS annual limit. Filling the rest of this space will either decrease your taxable income today with pre-tax contributions or allow your investments to grow tax-free with Roth contributions.

The final tax-advantaged vehicle you may have available through an employer is the after-tax (non-Roth) 401k. This account enables a technique referred to as the mega backdoor Roth, which is aptly named for the mega bucks you can stash in tax-advantaged space. This is not available in most work-based plans currently, but if your employer offers it, you have a huge tax advantage. There are two requirements that must be available in your 401k plan to enable the mega backdoor Roth:

1. After-tax (non-Roth) contributions beyond the individual limit
2. In-service distributions so you can put your funds in a Roth IRA or Roth 401k

The premise of the mega backdoor Roth is that while individuals can only contribute up to $19,500 to their 401k in 2020, the total contribution limit (combined individual and employer) is $57,000. If your employer's 401k plan allows after-tax contributions, you can effectively fill the gap between the individual limit and the total limit. This money is then distributed either to your Roth IRA or Roth 401k so it can grow tax-free, like any other Roth contribution.

For example, an employee earning $120,000 annually contributes the maximum $19,500 to the pre-tax 401k. The company provides an employer match of $7,200. That is a total contribution of $26,700, leaving another $30,300 that can be contributed to the mega backdoor Roth before hitting the total limit. That is over five times the amount that can normally be contributed to a Roth IRA, so this is a powerful benefit if you have a high saving rate.

One final space that can be used to further reduce taxable income is a 529 plan if you would like to save for college for you or your children (or anyone else, if you're feeling generous). Contributions to 529 plans are not deductible at the federal level, but they are for many states, and withdrawals for qualified education costs are tax-free. By contributing to 529 plans, you can reduce your state tax bill and allow for untaxed investment growth. However, you should be cautious not to overcontribute to a 529 due to the 10% penalty for withdrawals not used for college. For more details on 529 plans and your specific state, see the Boglehead wiki page for 529 plans.

5. Early repayment of high-interest debt

At this point, you have exhausted your tax-advantaged space, so your remaining decisions come down to optimizing risk and return rather than tax considerations. Paying down debt early and investing in regular taxable investment accounts are interchangeable in priority depending on your debt interest rates and personal preferences.

If you have student loans or other debt at 5% interest or more, paying them off early is a guaranteed return that is surely worth taking instead of investing in regular taxable accounts. However, if your debt is more in the 2-4% range, the choice comes down to personal preference. Would you rather lock in a guaranteed 3% return by paying down your debt or take some risk in the stock market, which has historically returned about 9% nominal over the long run? Personally, I would continue to invest in the market rather than pay off 3% interest debt early, knowing that on average, my investments will earn me a higher return in the long run. But there are also psychological benefits from freeing yourself of debt and simplifying your finances. Ultimately, either decision is financially savvy, so choose what feels right to you.

6. Regular taxable investment accounts

Regular taxable investment accounts are last on the list because they offer no tax benefits. You cannot deduct contributions from your income, and you must pay tax on gains and dividends. In addition to being a last stop for retirement investing, regular taxable accounts are the best spot for short-to-medium-term goals, such as saving for a car or down payment on a house. You can open a regular taxable account with the same brokerage firm that holds your IRA, such as Fidelity, Vanguard, or Schwab. If you're just getting started investing, they each have helpful walkthroughs to ensure you open the right type of account.

Optimizing your investment account usage may seem less exciting than picking individual funds, but it will likely have a larger impact on your portfolio performance. To illustrate, let's look at an example of two investors: Olivia, who follows the recommended order above, and Terry, who decided not to bother with this and just invests in regular taxable accounts. Both Olivia and Terry earn $120,000 annually living in Houston, but their strategies put them in very different financial positions.

Pre-tax Investments		
	Olivia	Terry
401k contribution	$19,500	$0
Employer 401k match	$7,200	$0
Total pre-tax	$26,700	$0

Tax-free Investments		
	Olivia	Terry
HSA contribution	$3,500	$0

Roth Investments		
	Olivia	Terry
Backdoor Roth IRA	$6,000	$0
Mega backdoor Roth	$22,500	$0
Total Roth	$28,500	$0

Regular Taxable Investments		
	Olivia	Terry
Regular taxable	$0	$46,000

Financial Overview		
	Olivia	Terry
Salary	$120,000	$120,000
Expenses	$45,000	$45,000
Income tax	$23,500	$29,000
Total investment	$58,700	$46,000
Total investment value after 30 years*	$406,000	$298,000

*Assuming investments earn 7% annual real return over 30 years, 15% capital gains tax, 20% effective income tax

Olivia and Terry work the same job and put in the same hours at the office. They earn the same income and have the same living expenses. Yet Olivia will have an **extra $108,000** available to her in retirement **for each year** she follows these saving and investment strategies. This is because Olivia leveraged all of her tax-advantaged space to reduce her income taxes today, allowing her to save more, and to reduce taxes on her future investment gains. If it took Olivia 10 hours total to read this chapter then set up and manage her accounts as described, that means she earned $10,000 an hour for that work. Not a bad hourly rate!

This is also something to consider when looking to switch jobs to a new company. Different companies have very different 401k plans, spanning the spectrum from no plan offered, to a 401k with no match, to a generous match and the ability to do mega backdoor Roth contributions. As the above example shows, this can make a difference of tens of thousands of dollars, so you should consider this alongside base salary in your decision-making process.

In summary, setting your asset allocation and putting your money in the right spot should be your first two priorities as an investor. With those two complete, we'll now discuss how to choose the individual funds that will help you earn more money passively than you ever have in your career.

CHAPTER 7

Invest in the market

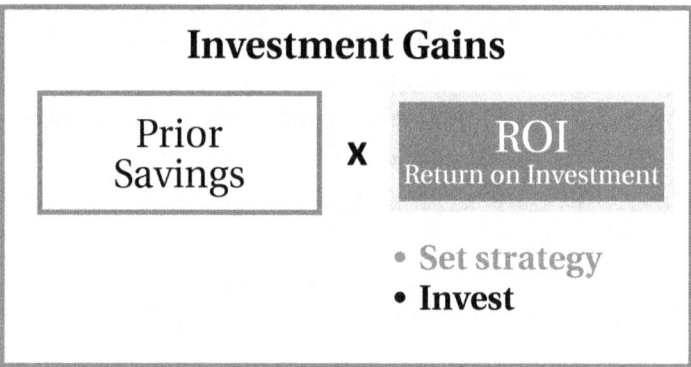

You've set your investment strategy, and the last step remaining to optimize your ROI is to pour some money in. It's the moment you've been waiting for – time for me to reveal the secret behind my hot stock picks that made me a 30-year-old millionaire!

Unfortunately, if that's what you're looking for, you're reading the wrong book. I won't be channeling Jim Cramer from *Mad Money* and ranting about which dozen stocks to buy and sell. In fact, I, like many other millionaires, **have never owned an individual company stock**.

This section is all about picking your individual *funds*, not your individual *stocks*. This is because the key to reliable wealth accumulation using stocks and bonds is to create a diversified portfolio that closely tracks overall market returns.

But why settle for market returns? Can't smart people spend

some time doing research and outperform the market average? The short answer is no. The long answer involves an explanation of the Efficient Market Hypothesis. This theory states that the market is efficient, meaning it is correctly priced based on all available information, and it is essentially impossible to beat market returns when adjusting for risk.

Of course, no market in the real world is 100% efficient. Inefficiency in the sports betting market enabled me to build a statistical model that priced more accurately than the sportsbooks. However, the stock market is an entirely different animal, with trillions of dollars continuously flowing through it to ensure pricing inadequacies are quickly corrected.

There are two ways to beat any market:

1. Leverage information the market doesn't have
2. Leverage the publicly available information better than the market

When investing in publicly traded stocks and bonds, the first method is called insider trading and is illegal. I recommend avoiding that so you can enjoy a fruitful retirement outside of jail.

The second is exceedingly difficult, bordering on impossible, for an individual investor. Massive financial conglomerates like Goldman Sachs and J.P. Morgan spend billions of dollars on world-class analysts and algorithms to exploit even the slightest edge in the market. And they do so using sub-second latency to execute trades immediately as information becomes available. To beat the market, you must somehow beat these companies without any of their advantages.

So, the bad news is that consistently beating the market is virtually impossible for you as an individual investor. But the good news is that you can earn market returns, which are more than enough to make you a millionaire.

Use low-cost passive index funds

Creating a diversified portfolio to replicate market returns used to be difficult and expensive. Individual investors would have to either pay a brokerage a large fee to invest in actively managed funds promising diversification or purchase a slew of stocks and bonds outright, which required constantly rebalancing between funds. Luckily for us, this problem was solved by Jack Bogle, founder of Vanguard and original champion of the low-cost index fund. Many other brokerages have followed suit, and passively earning market returns is now easier and cheaper than ever.

Many people think of earning market returns as earning *average* returns, and no one wants to be "just average." But the truth is quite the contrary; if your portfolio replicates overall market performance, you will be in the upper echelon of investment performance.

I mentioned previously how difficult it is to beat the market. Not only is it nearly impossible for individual investors, it's nearly impossible for the people who invest for a living: professional fund managers. According to the S&P Indices Versus Active (SPIVA) scorecard, almost 95% of actively managed funds fail to outperform their benchmark indexes over a 15-year period after accounting for fees.

So how can *you* earn above average returns? Simply invest in the market using low-cost passive index funds, and you'll beat 95% of professional money managers. These index funds will not only give you better returns, but also reduced volatility in your performance. Index funds typically hold hundreds or thousands of stocks or bonds. These individual holdings are not perfectly correlated, meaning they can move in different directions. For example, if Apple stock falls 3% in a day, Visa stock might rise 5% to offset it. Thus, passive index funds provide better diversification in addition to higher returns than their actively managed counterparts.

I've now explained the concept and shown with data why passive index funds are superior, but you may still be skeptical. This is not surprising, as the natural tendency of smart, driven people is to figure out ways to optimize and do more. You might want to start researching which active funds can consistently beat the market. Alright, if you insist, here's an active fund you can't pass up.

The Sequoia Fund (SEQUX) was founded by friends of Warren Buffett in 1970 to outperform the stock market. Their strategy is a simple one: invest in great businesses at reasonable prices. The fund managers accomplish this by doing exhaustive primary research, ignoring fads, and sticking to their principles. An investment of $10,000 in the fund at its inception would be worth $3.9 million today, while investing that $10,000 in the S&P 500 would be worth only $1.0 million. The fund has done this all while also taking less risk, measured by an indicator called beta, and has been recognized as one of the top funds over the last 4 decades. Here is a graph of more recent performance compared with that of Vanguard's Total Stock Market index fund.

As you can see, Sequoia fared better during the 2008-2009 crash, falling only 34% while the total market fell 42%. It also outgrew the market during the rebound. So, your choice is simple: invest in a market index fund and get average returns or invest in Sequoia to increase your returns while also minimizing your downside. What do you say?

Normally when making a decision like this, it will take years to find out if you chose correctly. Luckily, the data I presented above was a snapshot in time from mid-2015, so we can now fast-forward and see what's happened.

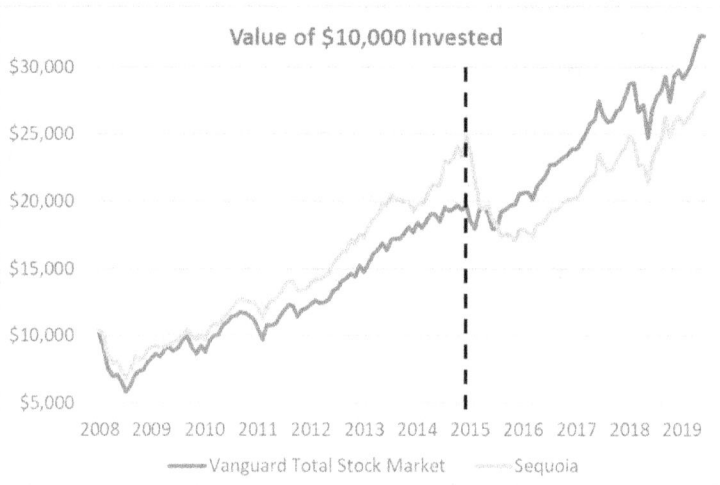

Ouch. If you invested in Sequoia, you're not feeling too great right now. $10,000 invested in the Sequoia Fund in mid-2015 would have dropped in value to under $6,900 one year later, while the total market continued its steady rise. Sequoia's performance was so bad that investors withdrew nearly $1 billion from the fund. Sequoia's management firm ran out of cash and forced shareholders to redeem "in kind," meaning investors had to pay taxes themselves to preserve company cash (which, while legal, is a sign of desperation).

After this collapse, the fund rebounded somewhat but has still significantly trailed performance of the total market. $10,000 invested in Sequoia in mid-2015 would be worth $11,100 at the start of 2020, while the same money invested in the total market would be worth $16,400. That's an 11% gain for Sequoia and a 64% gain for the total market.

The lesson from this example is that there are actively managed funds that look very attractive based on past performance, but that is no guarantee of future performance. Nearly all active funds will regress to the mean and fail to outperform the market in the long run.

The reason you will commonly find these often relatively new funds that *seem* to beat the market is because of something called survivorship bias. Every stock has about a 50% chance of over- or under-performing the market over a short time period. That means if I pick 100 stocks at random to invest in for a year, I expect 50 of them to look like solid picks.

The same principle applies to mutual funds. If I'm a professional fund manager and create 100 funds of stocks picked completely at random, 50 of these funds should "beat the market" before considering fees. When I add in the 2% fee I'm charging you to randomly pick stocks, about 40 funds still remain that beat the market in the first year. As the fund manager, I then kill off the 60 funds that underperformed and no longer offer those. The next year I advertise my 40 funds that beat the market. Of those 40, 15 beat the market by random chance once again. I repeat this process for 5 years, continuing to kill off the losing funds in the process, and voila! I now have a managed fund that has beaten the market for 5 years straight. As an investor, you only hear about the 1 fund that "survived" and beat the market, not the 99 funds that underperformed and were discontinued.

If you're tempted by the recent performance of an actively managed fund, just remember that you could do the same and save yourself some expenses by picking stocks with a magic 8-ball. Or you could follow this chapter's advice and invest in index funds. It may go against your natural tendency to take action, but when it comes to investing, lazier really is better.

Do it yourself

Hopefully now you're sold on investing in low-cost passive index funds and want to know the best way to move forward. There are two basic types of index funds that will suit your purpose.

- **Mutual funds** are essentially pools of money managed by investment companies that select a mix of stocks, bonds, and other securities in which to invest. They have a fund prospectus that articulates the fund's goal, such as to track the performance of the total U.S. stock market. Mutual funds can be either actively or passively managed.
- **Exchange-Traded Funds (ETFs)** also hold a collection of stocks, bonds, and other securities, but are traded directly by shareholders on the stock exchange, rather than purchased from the issuing company. ETFs typically track a market index and are passively managed.

The decision between mutual funds and ETFs is not a critical one, but ETFs have a slight edge for a few reasons. They typically have somewhat lower expense ratios and, since most major brokerages have eliminated trading fees, have no trading costs. ETFs also have more selection available at a given brokerage, which can be useful for tax-loss harvesting (which I'll explain in detail later). For example, if you have a brokerage account at Fidelity, you can purchase ETFs offered by Fidelity, Vanguard, Schwab, and more at no cost. This is also useful if you decide to change brokerage companies, as you can simply transfer your ETFs, which is often not possible with mutual funds. Finally, ETFs are more tax-efficient because they distribute less realized capital gains that you must pay taxes on.

In summary, if you have no reason to pick one or the other, go with ETFs, at least in your regular taxable account. The main reason you'd invest in a mutual fund instead is if you don't have a corresponding ETF available in your account, as you'll see in the sample portfolios below. All ETFs can be purchased at any large brokerage, so your choice in brokerage company can be based on any mutual funds you want or any other reason you might have to go with a specific firm. I personally use Fidelity, as it has individual HSA accounts and a solid Solo 401k setup, a combination that no other top brokerage has.

To help you put this advice into practice, some sample portfolios using funds from Vanguard, Fidelity, and Schwab are shown below. The funds in a given row are interchangeable. Expense ratios are provided for each fund in parentheses, current as of early 2020. Expense ratios frequently change, so these may be outdated when you are reading this (a quick Google search will return current expense ratios). That is fine; the purpose is to show which types of funds tend to be more expensive. However, these are all great, low-cost options. The most expensive fund shown has an expense ratio of 0.12%, meaning you will pay only $120 in fees per year for a portfolio of $100,000. Actively managed funds with broker fees can easily exceed 2.0% ratios, costing you $2,000 on the same portfolio.

	Extremely simple 1-fund portfolio		
Asset class	Vanguard	Fidelity	Schwab
Diverse Single Fund	Target Retirement (0.12%)	Fidelity Freedom (0.12%)	Schwab Target Index (0.08%)

First up is the extremely simple 1-fund portfolio, where you simply put all of your investments in a target retirement fund. These target retirement funds are typically not available in ETF format, so you'll need to go with mutual funds. The primary advantage of this portfolio is that it's the simplest approach, requiring virtually zero research or maintenance. Disadvantages include slightly higher fees (still only up to $120 a year on a $100,000 portfolio) and foregoing some tax avoidance techniques I'll explain in detail later. If you have been waiting or anxious about investing because it seems too complex, put your savings in a target retirement fund now and beat 95% of professional money managers.

| Very simple 2-fund portfolio ||||
Asset class	Vanguard	Fidelity	Schwab
Total World Equites	Total World Stock ETF VT (0.09%)	N/A	N/A
Bonds	Total Bond Market ETF BND (0.04%)	U.S. Bond Index FXNAX (0.025%)	U.S. Aggregate Bond Index ETF SCHZ (0.04%)

Next is the very simple 2-fund portfolio holding total world equities and bonds. This portfolio has the advantage of being another simple approach, while also allowing for customization of your equity and bond allocation. For example, if you want to maximize returns over a long horizon with 95% equities, you can do that with a 2-fund portfolio but not with a target retirement fund. One disadvantage of this portfolio is that it requires some maintenance work. You must pay attention to how your asset allocation shifts over time due to market performance and rebalance to return to your desired allocation.

| Simple, Lowest Cost 3-Fund Portfolio ||||
Asset class	Vanguard	Fidelity	Schwab
Domestic Equites	Total Stock ETF VTI (0.03%)	ZERO Total Market FZROX (0.00%)	U.S. Broad Market ETF SCHB (0.03%)
Intl. Equities	Total Intl. Stock ETF VXUS (0.09%)	ZERO Intl. Index FZILX (0.00%)	Intl. Equity Index ETF SCHF (0.06%)
Bonds	Total Bond Market ETF BND (0.04%)	U.S. Bond Index FXNAX (0.025%)	U.S. Aggregate Bond Index ETF SCHZ (0.04%)

Last but not least, the 3-fund portfolio is still simple and has the lowest cost. This portfolio consists of domestic equities, international equities, and bonds. The primary advantage of this approach is cost, with expense ratios at or near 0.00%, and full customization of asset allocation. This is important if you want a domestic bias like most investors have. This portfolio also has great potential for tax optimization due to several interchangeable funds for each of the three classes. The disadvantage of this approach is the required maintenance to keep asset allocation in check and take advantage of those tax opportunities. If you are a sophisticated investor, this is likely the approach you want to take.

Hopefully after seeing just how simple it can be to build your own investment portfolio, you've started to question the value of financial advisors. To be blunt, most financial advisors are a complete rip-off.

When I tell people I'm writing a personal finance book, I normally get one of two reactions. The first is general interest, asking what my main points are, etc. The second is "that's nice, but I don't really know anything about finance. I have a money guy that takes care of that stuff." I always cringe when I hear that, because it likely means they are being taken advantage of.

Financial advisors typically do no more than what you've already learned in this book, and they charge a pretty penny to do it. The worst culprits, high-fee firms like Edward Jones, cater to people who are looking for a "money guy" to handle everything. They charge a fee every year based on Assets Under Management (AUM), meaning that your advisor is paid a percentage of your portfolio every year, on top of the fees of the underlying fund. For example, an advisor might charge a 2% AUM fee, so if your funds are invested in a Vanguard Target Retirement fund with a 0.12% expense ratio, you'll pay 2.12% total in fees every year. That essentially increases your annual fees by 1,600%!

However, many advisors don't use low-cost funds like a Vanguard Target Retirement fund. Instead, they channel clients to actively managed funds with higher fees because they get more commission for doing so. As previously discussed, not only do these funds have higher fees; they also have worse performance than index funds. Numbers like 2% can sound small and harmless, but the effect on your portfolio over time can be devastating. To illustrate, let's look at an example with two investors. Both start with a $100,000 portfolio and save $20,000 a year for the next 30 years. Both investors want to keep things simple and not have to think about investing. One does this using a Vanguard Target Retirement fund. The other gives their money to an advisor charging a 1.5% AUM fee and using an actively managed fund with a 1.3% expense ratio.

	Vanguard Target Retirement	Advisor-Managed Portfolio
AUM Fee	0.00%	1.50%
Average Fund Fee	0.12%	1.30%
Annual Return	6.00%	6.00%
Starting Portfolio	$100,000	$100,000
Annual Saving	$20,000	$20,000
Portfolio After 30 Years	$2,103,322	$1,240,215

After 30 years, the investor using the advisor has 59% of the wealth as the do-it-yourself investor. That's nearly a $900,000 difference! This example is not a hyperbole; it is common for advisors to charge fees in this range. So, unless you want to donate nearly half of your wealth to your financial advisor, you should manage your own investments.

If you're currently using one of these high-fee advisors, don't be too hard on yourself. These companies are experts at hiding fees and making people complacent, and there are millions of others who have made the same decision. Luckily, it's a fairly painless process to correct this. You can open an account at Fidelity, Vanguard, or Schwab and tell them you'd like to transfer all your assets from your current advisor. They'll walk you through the process from there, and **you won't even have to talk to your current advisor**. And if you absolutely insist on paying someone to talk you through your investment decisions, look for an advisor who charges hourly rather than by AUM or go with a lower-cost firm like Vanguard Advisory Services.

Now that we've covered creating your investment portfolio on your own, let's look at how you can manage these investments to maximize return.

Minimize tax liability

You were probably hoping we were done talking about taxes after the fund placement section. Sorry to disappoint, but taxes are an extremely important part of investing. There's just one more tax topic to cover – how to minimize taxes in your regular taxable brokerage accounts.

The first priority here is to follow the advice from the fund placement section and fill your tax-advantaged space first. However, assuming your saving rate gets high enough, you will need to invest in regular taxable accounts. To do this optimally, you'll want a broad understanding of how investments are taxed.

Bond funds typically pay back investors in the form of interest payments but can also earn returns through increasing prices, referred to as capital gains. Stock funds are essentially the inverse, primarily adding value through capital gains while also providing some direct payments to investors in the form of dividends.

Interest payments from bonds and dividends from stocks are normally taxed as regular income, the same as your work salary. However, some dividends are considered "qualified dividends," meaning they are taxed as capital gains rather than regular income. Capital gains are taxed at a special, *lower* tax rate than other sources of income. This tax is only paid when the price at which you sell a fund is higher than the price you paid for it. You do not pay tax at all until you sell, at which point your gains are "realized." You have "unrealized" gains which are *not* taxed until you sell. And if you sell at a loss (the price is lower than what you paid for it), you actually get a tax *credit*, reducing the amount you owe the IRS.

Putting all this together, bond funds generate a stream of income that is taxed at regular income tax rates, while stock funds do not generate much taxable income until you sell. Additionally, ETFs holding stocks and bonds are generally taxed just like their underlying assets. There are many more intricacies involved in investment taxation, but this foundation is all you need to make smart decisions. Your brokerage company will provide you with documents each year that can be imported into your tax filing software or given to your tax preparer to take care of it for you.

Now, how should you use this information? In general, you want the bond portion of your portfolio to be in tax-advantaged space, so you won't have to pay the higher income taxes from bond interest payments. That means if your allocation is 90% equities and 10% bonds, you should buy all your bonds in your 401k or Roth IRA and only invest in equities in your regular taxable account. This will result in your individual accounts not reflecting your desired asset allocation, but that is fine as long as your portfolio as a whole adds up. For example, a total portfolio of $100,000 split across regular taxable and tax-advantaged retirement account would look like this:

	Equities	Bonds
Regular Taxable	$ 50,000	$ -
Tax-Advantaged	$ 40,000	$ 10,000
Total	$ 90,000	$ 10,000

Within the equity asset class, the placement of domestic vs. international depends on your income tax bracket. International equities get a credit for foreign tax paid, while domestic equities typically have a higher proportion of qualified dividends. Ultimately the difference between the two in terms of tax efficiency is small and likely not worth worrying about. If you are really curious, you can check out the Bogleheads forum thread "Relative tax efficiency including Foreign Tax Credit" to see how to calculate tax efficiency for your individual situation.

The next tax-saving tip is to avoid realizing capital gains until you really need the money. Assuming you follow this book's advice and have an equity-heavy portfolio, most of your investment gains will come from capital gains, which are only taxed when realized. When investing for retirement over a long timeframe, you will likely have significantly more in capital gains than you invested as your basis. You want to avoid paying capital gains tax today for two main reasons. The first is that most people are in a lower tax bracket in retirement and will pay lower capital gains tax, possibly even 0%. The second reason is that, as accountants like to say, "a tax deferred is a tax avoided." Due to the time value of money, even if you pay the same tax rate in retirement, you would rather pay that tax as late as possible to allow your money to grow.

My final investing tax tip is to take advantage of a powerful tax avoidance technique called **tax loss harvesting**. Tax loss harvesting is the most complex topic covered in this book. If you can effectively use it, you are officially an elite investor and will see performance far better than your peers. I mentioned earlier that if equities you purchase increase in price, you have capital gains. On the flip side, if they decrease in price, that is considered a **capital loss**. Normally, losses are bad. You want your investments to grow, not shrink. However, you'll inevitably experience losses at some point, and you can make the most of those losses (especially during big market downturns) to lower your tax obligation.

The basic idea behind tax loss harvesting is that when you have a loss on a specific fund, you sell it and shift the money into a similar-but-not-identical fund. This gives you a realized capital loss for tax purposes while still maintaining your desired asset allocation with the new purchase. The advantage of doing this is that capital losses offset capital gains in a given year, and any excess losses can be deducted from your taxable income up to a $3,000 annual cap. Losses above that cap can be carried forward perpetually to reduce income in future years, meaning realized capital losses can lower your income taxes for years to come.

Here's an example to help make this more real. You invest $10,000 in the Vanguard Total Stock ETF. The market falls 15% over the next 6 months, bringing your investment down to $8,500. You sell the Vanguard Total Stock ETF and buy $8,500 of the Schwab U.S. Broad Market ETF (a similar but not identical fund). This results in a realized $1,500 capital loss while still maintaining your allocation in domestic equities. When you do your tax return for the year, you can deduct $1,500 of regular income. If your effective income tax rate is 40%, you just saved $600 in taxes this year.

That is a small example of tax loss harvesting; its power really shows when used with a large portfolio. Investment services firm First Quadrant performed a study in which it simulated returns over 25 years to measure the impact of tax loss harvesting. They found that by realizing losses, the average portfolio saw a 14% advantage in returns versus a pure buy-and-hold strategy in typical market conditions. Essentially, by leveraging tax loss harvesting, you are earning an additional 14% in investment returns without taking any additional risk.

To best enable tax loss harvesting, follow the sample 3-fund portfolio. This allows you to harvest losses of either domestic or international equities with plenty of similar alternative funds to switch into. The detailed mechanics of tax loss harvesting are beyond the scope of this book, so when you're ready, check out the Bogleheads forum post TLH for Absolute Dummies and their Tax Loss Harvesting wiki page.

Stay the course

While the last section highlighted the actions you can take to minimize taxes, this section returns to the ever-important *inaction* of investing. When you set your investment strategy, including asset allocation, it is critical to stick with it. You want to avoid overreacting to market swings, and, as Jack Bogle often said, "stay the course."

Analyzing the market crash of 2008 is a great way to illustrate the importance of this concept. Let's consider three investors during this timeframe:

- Dan invested in a few tech stocks like Pets.com during the dot-com boom and saw his wealth skyrocket before losing almost everything when the market dropped. He since learned the merits of diversifying through index funds to

prevent this from happening again, but he was still nervous about losing it all. Because of this, Dan sold his stocks during the crash of 2008 and did not feel comfortable re-entering the market until two years later.
- Mark is a financial analyst who is confident in his ability to predict the stock market and avoid downswings to maximize profit. He brags about how he has a "sense for the market" and was able to react quickly to miraculously avoid the 2008 crash. He sensed another downswing in 2010 that did not pan out but feels he really didn't miss much growth.
- Stacy is a buy-and-hold investor who does not believe she can time the market. She invests $500 from each paycheck and doesn't pay attention to market buzz since she's investing for the long-term. She did not sell any stock during the 2008 crash.

All three of these investors had $100,000 in total stock market index funds in late 2006 leading up to the 2008 crash. They also saved $1,000 each month to add to their portfolios. Let's see how they fared.

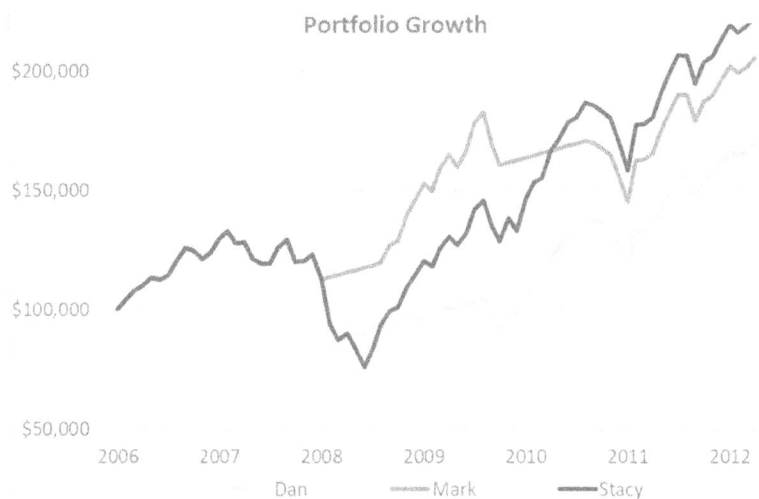

As you can see, Mark avoided the market crash, but Stacy ends up on top! How can that be?

To put it simply, **time in the market beats timing the market**.

Although Mark dodged the drop in late 2008 and early 2009, he missed out on some nice returns from mid-2010 to 2011 by incorrectly predicting another downswing. While Stacy saw significant losses from the crash, she stayed in the market and reaped the full rewards of the recovery. At the end of 2012, her portfolio value was $223,000: 8% higher than Mark's.

Mark vs. Stacy illustrates how even great market timers lose out to steady investors. But Dan shows how big the gap can be when timing efforts aren't quite as lucky. In 2006, Dan had a $100,000 portfolio and contributed another $76,000 from then until the end of 2012. However, his investments lost him money, resulting in an ending balance of $170,000. That is over $50,000 lower than Stacy, who took no action at all. Most of us aren't miracle-workers like Mark, so attempting to time the market will likely result in poor investment performance like Dan's.

To avoid that temptation, think of investing as a simple monthly activity that you schedule. Set aside an hour each month to check for tax loss harvesting opportunities, invest newly available savings according to your target asset allocation, and reinvest dividends and interest you've received. There is no benefit to "checking in on your investments" or looking to make portfolio tweaks outside that monthly cadence.

This will also help you to invest money as it becomes available. The 2008 crash example shows the negative impacts of market timing. Withholding money from investing because you believe the market is "overvalued" or you want to "wait for the next dip" is no better than what Dan did by selling his stock. Stick to your investment plan, invest what you can during your monthly session, and remember that time in the market beats timing the market.

When you invest more money each month, you will want to allocate your new contributions to return as close as possible to your target asset allocation. For example, let's say my target asset allocation is 90% equities and 10% bonds, and I have a $100,000 portfolio. At the end of the month, I see that my equity balance has risen with the market and is now at $95,000, while my bonds remained steady at $10,000. My asset allocation is now 90.4% equities and 9.6% bonds. If I have $2,000 to invest this month, I should allocate $1,300 to equities and $700 to bonds. This will bring my total balance to $96,300 in equities and $10,700 in bonds, back to my target 90/10 allocation. This helps you retain the risk that you set as part of your strategy and also helps improve your returns by forcing you to "buy low" when the market has dropped.

In addition to this monthly process, it is worthwhile to do a deeper dive at the end of the year to check in on your financial progress. Was your saving rate what you expected it to be or do you need to adjust your budget? Is your target asset allocation still appropriate for your investment horizon? Also, this annual check-in can be used to rebalance if your asset allocation has shifted too far away from your target to catch up using the monthly method above.

I have one final tip to make investing easy: look to consolidate your investment accounts as much as possible. For example, I have my work 401k, individual 401k, Roth IRA, HSA, and regular taxable account all at Fidelity. This means I have one place to log in and view my portfolio every month, making it very easy to rebalance. As mentioned previously, Vanguard and Schwab are also great brokerages for consolidation, but I chose Fidelity because it is the only one of the three with individual HSA accounts.

That is really all there is to investing: (1) set an appropriate asset allocation; (2) leverage your tax-advantaged accounts; (3) use low-cost index funds; (4) minimize tax liability; and (5) stay the course. If it's really as simple as I say, you may be wondering why investing is made to seem so intricate and expensive. The reason is that financial institutions and mainstream media make more money when people *believe* investing is complex.

Financial consultants, brokers, and otherwise-titled salespeople want to convince you that you need their advice or fund management, for which they will gladly take 1% or more of your assets every year. Brokerages want you to have a high volume of trading activity so they can collect fees directly or invest the money you have deposited with them. The media wants you to constantly tune in and view its advertisements, largely funded by the consultants and brokerages previously mentioned. Everyone wants you to think investing is hard so they can make more money off you.

By following the simple advice in this section, you can manage your own investments and earn returns better than 95% of professional money managers. With an optimized portfolio, you will soon earn more in passive investment returns than you've ever made in your career.

How I did it

Investing played a key role in my journey to become a millionaire at age 28. Over that accumulation timespan, my net worth increased by over $200,000 due to investment gains. While my total income during that time was much higher, I would not have attained this milestone without investing wisely.

I was fortunate to get an early start on investing when I was bagging groceries in high school. While I didn't understand the power of compound returns at the time, I did understand one thing: free money. My dad explained that the 401k match offered by the grocery store was free money, so I contributed enough to get a whopping $73 company match. That money has since more than doubled, and I never looked back on saving for retirement.

Shortly after starting my career post-college, I read the *Bogleheads' Guide to Investing* and learned how important it was to use tax-advantaged accounts and low-cost index funds. While the target retirement fund to which I'd been contributing was nice and simple, I decided to further optimize my investments and buy the funds individually. This meant I also needed to set an intentional asset allocation. I landed on 100% equities, split 70/30 between domestic/international. I knew I had a long investment horizon and that short-term drops wouldn't bother me, so I chose to maximize my long-term returns.

The final evolution in my investing journey came when I learned the more advanced techniques of tax loss harvesting and the mega backdoor Roth. At this point, I realized that picking funds is the easy part of investing, and minimizing taxes is what really differentiates investment returns.

To show how I leveraged the concepts of the past two chapters, let's take an in-depth look at the year 2018. This was after Rachel and I had significantly increased our incomes but before we had access to the mega backdoor Roth through her employer, so we deposited more into regular taxable accounts. Here is the full breakdown of where our money went that year:

2018	
Combined W-2 Salary	$265,000
Other Income	$13,000
401k Contribution	$38,000
Employer Match	$13,250
Backdoor Roth IRA	$11,000
HSA	$6,900
Taxable Income	$233,100
Income Tax	$60,400
Expenses	$61,000
Total Pre-Tax Investment	$51,250
Total Roth Investment	$11,000
Total No-Tax Investment	$6,900
Total Regular Taxable	$100,700

It's also worth noting that the market took a significant dip in late 2018, enabling us to tax loss harvest in our regular taxable account. We sold some domestic equities and purchased a similar fund to realize the losses and reduce our taxable income by $3,000 in 2018 and a few additional years in the future.

I mentioned that my asset allocation is 100% equities, with a 70/30 domestic/international split. Theoretically, that should only require 2 funds to execute. However, there are limited 401k fund choices and tax loss harvesting opportunities that add to your number of funds. Here is a snapshot of Rachel and my total portfolio as of year-end 2018.

Total Portfolio		
Asset class	Amount	Portfolio %
Domestic equities	$ 445,000	70.1%
Intl. equities	$ 190,000	29.9%
Bonds	$ -	-

Blake Work 401k		
Asset class	Name	Amount
Domestic Equities	Fidelity Total Market Index	$18,000

Blake Solo 401k		
Asset class	Name	Amount
Domestic Equities	Vanguard Total Stock	$23,000
Intl. Equities	Vanguard Total Intl Stock	$190,000

Blake Roth IRA		
Asset class	Name	Amount
Domestic Equities	Vanguard Total Stock	$74,000

Blake HSA		
Asset class	Name	Amount
Domestic Equities	Vanguard Total Stock	$9,000

Rachel Work 401k		
Asset class	Name	Amount
Domestic Equities	Vanguard Institutional Index	$96,000

Rachel Roth IRA		
Asset class	Name	Amount
Domestic Equities	Fidelity Total Zero Market Index	$56,000

Joint Regular Taxable		
Asset class	Name	Amount
Domestic Equities	Vanguard Total Stock Market ETF	$135,000
Domestic Equities	Schwab U.S. Broad Market ETF	$34,000

Of course, the stock market has short-term fluctuations; it does not go up every year. After propelling me past $1 million net worth, my investment portfolio suddenly dropped under $850,000 in early 2020 due to the pandemic. However, I followed my investment plan and stayed the course. I took advantage of the tax loss harvesting opportunity to lower my taxes and maintained my asset allocation, continuing to invest more money in the market after every paycheck. By the middle of the year, this strategy had paid off. My portfolio was larger than ever, and my recent investments already had significant gains.

Your investments won't be in the green every day, but if you do as I did and stick to your plan, you will come out ahead in the long run.

SECTION IV

Reap the rewards

With your personal net worth equation optimized, it's time to recognize and capitalize on your financial success.

CHAPTER 8

Savor the journey

The journey to accumulate wealth is an exhilarating one, and you'll likely want to dive in right away. That is a great attitude to have, but as you're cutting your expenses and putting in the extra hours to earn more money, you also want to ensure that you savor the journey. You don't have to sacrifice your life today for the potential of happiness in the future. Your net worth equation is only optimized when you're accumulating wealth while also living the life you desire.

My friend Al is an extreme example of this. Al was earning good money in his tech job in DC and living as frugally as it gets. His diet largely consisted of frozen pizza and ramen noodles, and he lived with two roommates in a two-bedroom apartment. He was the one without the bedroom, sleeping on a futon in the living room. When he was explaining his financial situation to me, he had already accumulated $400,000 in net worth and was looking to hit $1 million as quickly as possible so he could quit his job and move to a lower-cost area. He didn't really know what he wanted to do with his time after that; he just knew that he wanted to be as far from his current high-pressure job as possible.

Al was trapped in a false dichotomy. He saw his only two options: continuing to work in a toxic environment or saving every penny he earned to retire ASAP. In reality, because he had accumulated so much money so quickly, he now had endless options to choose from. Even if he didn't save another dollar for the next

30 years, his $400,000 portfolio invested in the stock market would likely grow to over $3,000,000. To enable that, all he needed to do was find work that could cover his modest living expenses.

After I explained this to Al (and he took a couple more months to actually believe it), he switched to remote work and moved close to family and friends in his home state of Texas. He now enjoys his work *and* his life, his portfolio is over $500,000, and he's significantly improved his standard meal.

Getting a solid start to your wealth accumulation journey, like Al did, gives you an incredible gift of optionality. When you have a significant investment portfolio, you drastically reduce your need to save in the future. This opens up a world of possibilities. You can look for more enjoyable, lower-paying work. You can go part-time. You can increase your expenses to finally take that trip you've been dreaming of.

There is no reason to delay granting yourself these privileges other than the outdated view of retirement in which you are supposed to work hard until you're 65 or 70 and then hope to enjoy a few years while your health permits it. Instead, put your money to use and improve your life satisfaction *today*. If you are off to a good start, you shouldn't worry too much if you make a decision to improve your life that sets back your retirement from age 45 to 47. Wouldn't you rather enjoy the next 10 years rather than have an extra two years of retirement?

There are three main tips I will offer to help you savor the journey: prioritize what's important, avoid burnout, and set realistic goals.

1. Prioritize what's important

This book is about money, so I'm not going to pretend money isn't important. Accumulating wealth is critical to living the life you want to live. But it isn't the only thing that matters. You must determine what else is important to you in life and ensure that you're prioritizing appropriately. For example, if family is important to you but you only see your daughter on weekends due to your long work hours, you need to assess whether your actions are aligned with your priorities.

Often, when a conflict arises between money and other high-priority aspects of life, it is due to your job. Since you will spend most of your waking hours at your job, choosing the right one is critical, and you should do adequate cost-benefit analysis. The primary benefit of work, at least for most people, is money. But there are also non-financial components to consider, such as whether the work is rewarding and enjoyable to you. The primary cost is your time. If your job demands long hours or for you to be available 24/7, the cost to you is much higher.

Remember that you hold the chips when negotiating to start a new job. There are likely hundreds of compatible employers you could choose from. So prioritize your happiness and don't settle for a less-than-ideal job just to save a little effort in the search.

Another potential cause of conflict in your life priorities is your spending. While reducing spending will help you achieve your financial goals, you should spend money on the things that make you happy. We talked earlier about an easy way to do this: prioritize spending on experiences, which studies have shown will increase your happiness more than buying things, which you inevitably get used to.

Following this advice during my own financial journey, I decided to prioritize my family and friends. I left my high-paying job in the Bay Area to move back to my true home of Chicago, sacrificing some of my upward salary mobility (and views of the ocean) to spend more time with loved ones. I also prioritized spending money on travel and some other random hobbies, like scooting around on my Vespa. All of these helped me keep balance and enjoy life while saving for my future.

2. Avoid burnout

Notice I'm saying to *avoid* burnout, not to *mitigate* it. That means you need to act before you're already burned out.

In case you're not familiar with the term, burnout is a state of emotional, physical, and mental exhaustion caused by excessive and prolonged stress. Early signs of burnout include a constant tired/drained feeling, lack of motivation, and a perpetual preoccupation with work. Becoming burned out will significantly hinder your long-term finances and reduce your life satisfaction. Working to exhaustion one year to make $200,000 isn't helpful if you have a mental breakdown and are unable to work the following year. In fact, you'll come out significantly ahead if you make half the income spread across two years, since your effective tax rate will be lower.

To avoid burnout, ensure you follow the guidance in the health section of this book, especially the advice to exercise regularly and get enough sleep. Both of these are proven to significantly reduce stress. Additionally, consider taking a longer hiatus from work to truly unwind more than is possible from a short vacation. To do this, after you've accumulated some wealth, check with HR if you can do a 6-month period of unpaid leave. You'll be surprised that many employers will honor this for their high performers, especially if you work at a large company.

Despite making efforts to avoid burnout, some jobs are simply more stressful than others. You can either accept this new norm or decide to move on to a new role. There is no shame in deciding that a job is not a good fit for you. I left a company after only 9 months to move to a lower-stress job in an industry with which I was more familiar. This made me happier at work and gave me more time to dedicate to my side hustles and see friends and family.

As you advance in your wealth accumulation journey, you can also assess whether the combination of your day job and side hustles is leading to burnout. You can mitigate this by finding a side hustle you enjoy or cutting back the amount of time you spend on it. For example, my side hustle of building sports betting predictive models made good money but took up an extra 25 hours a week on top of my day job. As my portfolio started to grow, I decided the time and risk of burnout was no longer worth it.

3. Set realistic goals

It's not fun to repeatedly fail. Set yourself up to succeed by setting realistic financial goals.

Becoming a millionaire by age 30 is something I realized was possible when I was 25 and set that as my personal financial goal. Most people have a lower starting point than I did. That's completely fine; it simply means you should adjust your goals based on your current financial position. If you're 50 years old and currently make $50,000 a year, you can set a goal to increase your income by 10% within the next year (either through a new job or a side hustle) and save 100% of the extra money. Regardless of what age you are and what stage of your career you're in, you can take steps now to accumulate wealth.

It's also important to recognize that financial success doesn't happen overnight. You can cut expenses relatively quickly, but it takes time to increase your income and for your investments to notably grow. Unless you currently have a net worth of $5, establishing a goal to double your net worth in the next month is setting yourself up for failure. Keep in mind that the average American under 45 has just $36,000 in net worth, so don't hesitate to set a financial goal in the thousands rather than the millions.

Additionally, be prepared to adjust your goals along the way. My original plan was to hit $1 million net worth and promptly retire to life of leisure. However, as I pursued that goal, I realized that I didn't want a life of leisure. I live for the chase and would be bored out of my mind if I was not aggressively pursuing a goal. Also, I want to have kids and take up some expensive hobbies like flying airplanes, which are not possible with a $1 million retirement portfolio at age 30. This decision not to retire turned out to be prudent given the 2020 market downturn.

That downturn exemplifies another reason you should adjust your goals along the way: it's impossible to predict your short-term investment performance. I set a net worth goal of $1 million by age 30 and hit it at 28…right before the stock market tanked and my net worth dropped by $200,000. These fluctuations happen, so I am instead focusing on my saving rate, with a goal of saving $150,000 per year over the next 5 years. Even ignoring investment returns, that will add another $750,000 in net worth, but I probably still won't retire. I'll see what I'm feeling passionate about at the time and set my next goal accordingly.

And, of course, I'll savor the journey along the way.

CHAPTER 9

Achieve financial independence

If you've followed the advice in the book so far, that means you've increased your income, kept your expenses in check, and invested your money so your net worth can grow while you sleep. And hopefully you've also enjoyed the journey. But what is the journey's end destination? How do you know when you've "won" the game of personal finance? For most people, that comes when you achieve financial independence.

This means that you can cover your expenses without relying on employment. You can choose how you spend your time, unrestricted from the constraints of a job. You can pursue the passions that bring the most fulfillment in life without worrying about generating income. It is a truly liberating position to be in, and the pinnacle of financial success.

You may have previously heard of financial independence through the increasingly popular FIRE (Financial Independence, Retire Early) movement. There was even a movie made about it in 2019: *Playing with FIRE* (not to be confused with the John Cena comedy *Playing with Fire*, rated an impressively bad 22% on Rotten Tomatoes). The core premise is to save a large portion of your income, sometimes above 50%, to retire early and live off small withdraws from an accumulated investment portfolio. FIRE seekers tend to be a bit extreme, but the principles are not much different than what has been outlined in this book.

Financial independence is the more important half of the FIRE acronym. The second half of FIRE, retiring early, is simply one option out of the many you have once you hit the financial independence milestone. While financially independent people have the ability to retire, many choose not to. Instead, they often continue to work so they can spend more in retirement or find work that is more meaningful to them.

Assuming you don't have other forms of passive income, you must be able to live off your portfolio for the rest of your life to become fully financially independent. To do this, your portfolio must hit a certain value to be able to cover your expenses for the rest of your life. We refer to this as your **number**.

Calculate your number

Let's look at an early retirement scenario: Gary is 50 years old with annual expenses of $40,000 per year. Gary's family has a typical health history, so it's possible he could live another 50 years (and he wants to be able to cover the expenses for those 50 years). Intuitively, you would say he needs $40,000 * 50 = $2,000,000 saved up.

Following that calculation, I have good news and bad news. The good news is that the amount Gary actually needs is significantly lower. The bad news is that calculating his real number is much more difficult. Because Gary's portfolio will continue to grow through compound returns, he doesn't need all the money he will ever spend at the time he retires. He needs to factor in his investment returns, inflation, and other sources of income like social security.

Rather than doing these calculations manually, many people use the simple calculators provided as part of 401k programs or talk to financial advisors. These often come back with some pretty crazy numbers. The most recent calculator I looked at told me I needed about $4 million to retire! If that was the case, less than 1% of Americans would ever reach retirement.

Luckily, the assumptions built into that calculator (and many others) are overly pessimistic. They assume returns lower than we've ever seen historically and no other income, such as social security. Once you change these assumptions, the number becomes much more reasonable.

The first step in calculating your number is to estimate your ongoing annual expenses. For now, it's okay if this number is just a ballpark estimate based on your prior years' spending. However, as you get closer to retirement and hitting your number, you should estimate more precisely to ensure you have everything covered.

Two big expenses to consider when entering retirement are health insurance and lifestyle changes. Because most Americans get health insurance through their employer, retiring (or even just cutting back to part-time) can result in a significant increase in costs. This can be mitigated by carefully managing taxable income in retirement, but it's not uncommon for early retirees to see their health expenditure double. Additionally, to accurately calculate your number, you must account for any lifestyle changes that will come in retirement. For older retirees, the change could be minimal; but if you plan to retire early and travel the world, you must include that in your annual expense projection.

Once you have a grasp on expenses, you then need to determine the other side of the finance equation: income. Will you be able to cover at least a portion of your expenses with income that will continue in retirement? This includes social security, pension payments, passive income from real estate, or any part-time work you plan to continue.

Social security and pensions are particularly useful because they pay out from a certain age for the remainder of your life, providing a form of longevity insurance. To ensure you qualify for social security benefits, you need to earn taxable income above a certain threshold for at least 10 years. This shouldn't be difficult to do, as the threshold is only $5,640 in 2020.

Any form of income you can maintain during retirement will drastically reduce your number, enabling you to retire earlier. For example, if you expect to have $50,000 in annual expenses in retirement and get $25,000 a year from social security, the amount you need to withdraw from your portfolio each year is cut in half. This cuts your retirement number in half, too.

After estimating your ongoing expenses and income in retirement, you can use some assumptions to estimate your number: how large your portfolio most be to reach financial independence. The simplest way to do this is to use a percentage rule of thumb. For example, you may have heard of the popular 4% rule. This rule provides a baseline for how much can be safely withdrawn from a portfolio to last a 30-year retirement. Based on the famous Trinity study, the rule states that a retiree can safely withdraw 4% of their portfolio in the first year of retirement and increase that withdrawal according to inflation each year. This has historically proven to survive a 30-year retirement with a near-100% success rate.

"Only 4%? You said the stock market earns 7% real returns! What gives?"

Even though your portfolio might average annual returns of 7% real, it is not safe to plan on withdrawing that much each year because of volatility. A major decrease in the early years of retirement leaves less money remaining to grow, hampering your returns.

For example, let's say you retire with a $1,000,000 portfolio, planning to spend 7% each year. In your first year of retirement, you spend $70,000 and the market plunges, resulting in a 30% loss in your investments. Factoring in your withdrawal and the market downturn, you are now left with $651,000 entering year two. Assuming you earn solid 8% returns from there on and continue to spend $70,000 per year, you will run out of money in year 17. At that point, you better hope you've been nice enough to your children for them to put you in a nursing home room with a window.

The 4% rule exists to reduce the risk that is inherent in volatile market returns. So someone with a $1,000,000 portfolio could withdraw $40,000 each year. However, this rule was developed for a 30-year retirement. If you plan on retiring early (or just living longer), 3.5% is a safer number to use for 50-year retirements, as Karsten Jeske showed in his "Safe Withdrawal Rate Series" on EarlyRetirementNow.com.

Let's return to our example of Gary, the 50-year-old retiree with $40,000 in annual expenses. Applying the 3.5% rule to Gary's $40,000 annual expenses, his retirement number would be $1,140,000 – significantly lower than the $2,000,000 we naively calculated earlier.

However, we did not include any income in retirement. Gary plans to continue to earn $10,000 a year until age 65 doing some consulting work, after which he will get $10,000 a year from social security. That decreases the amount he needs from his portfolio to $30,000 per year. Again using 3.5% to cover a 50-year retirement, that brings his number to $860,000. That's less than half of our original number and nearly $300,000 lower than when we excluded his retirement income. This illustrates the massive impact that additional income in retirement can make. This is why some people pursue what is called "Barista FI," in which they can quit their current job and switch to a lower-paying part-time job such as working as a barista at Starbucks (they also provide great health insurance).

This example was simple because Gary earned constant income throughout his retirement. Real life is unlikely to be so neat, which is where financial calculators come in handy. My favorite is FIREcalc, which allows you to input your projected expenses, portfolio size, asset allocation, retirement years, and variable income amounts to see how you would have fared in retirement across all historic scenarios dating back to 1871. You can then adjust the portfolio size to get to a retirement success rate that you are comfortable with. Fidelity also offers a solid calculator that you can save and retrieve later for free.

Clearly, calculating your number isn't easy. However, it shouldn't take long to get a reasonable estimate as your starting point using the 3.5% or 4% rule, which have traditionally been used to determine when you can safely retire. While these fixed percentage rules are effective at mitigating downside risk and ensuring you don't run out of money in retirement, they have one major flaw: they do not effectively leverage the upside of your investments. Sticking to a fixed withdrawal rate throughout a long retirement results in massive fluctuations in your ending portfolio depending on market performance. As finance guru Michael Kitces notes, half of the time, a FIRE retiree with a 3.5% withdrawal rate ends up with almost 10x their initial portfolio. Retiring for 40-50 years with $1 million and a 3.5% withdrawal rate, your portfolio has a good chance of growing to over $10 million!

Having all that extra money might not seem like a *problem*, but it's likely not that useful to you late in life (unless you're hoping to buy a private island). Instead, it means that you retired significantly later than you could have and will end up with a pile of cash with you in your coffin. You can help avoid the mistake of retiring too late by using a variable percentage withdrawal strategy rather than a fixed strategy like 3.5%.

The basic premise of a variable withdrawal strategy is that you can retire with a smaller portfolio if you are willing to make spending cuts during periods of market downturn. Thus, if you have flexibility in your spending or your income and modify them based on your investment performance, you can become financially independent much sooner.

A simple way to reap the benefits of this strategy is to split your ongoing expenses between core expenses that you need to live a satisfying life and luxury expenses that you could go without. If Gary, who earns $10,000 income throughout retirement, deems that $34,000 of his annual expenses are core expenses he doesn't want to sacrifice, while $6,000 are luxury expenses that he could ditch in a market downturn, his new number becomes

$24,000 / 3.5% = $686,000. That number is almost $200,000 lower than if he was using a fixed percentage method.

Again, Gary's example is pretty simple, but there are proven ways to optimize the variable withdrawal strategy to hit financial independence as early as possible. If you'd like to dive in more on the subject, the Bogleheads variable percentage withdrawal wiki page has more detail, including links to spreadsheets you can use to calculate your portfolio number and make adjustments to spending in retirement.

Following the techniques used in this example, I hope you find your number is lower than you suspected. I have found that many people on financial forums are overly conservative when calculating their numbers. Keep in mind that if you retire a bit early, you are simply risking having to decrease your spending or find another income source. If you retire too late, that lost time is gone.

Win the game

Once you've hit your financial independence number, it's time to celebrate: you've officially won the financial game!

You now have complete ownership of your time and limitless options of how to spend it. You could fully retire, either domestically with reasonable expenses, or go overseas and live like a king. You could pursue your true passion, regardless of whether it makes money, such as volunteering at your favorite charity. You could cut back on your work hours to spend more time with family and friends. You could join the expensive country club, buy a mansion, or do whatever other millionaire activities you want.

In reality, you'll likely do some combination of the above. The true beauty of financial independence is that it takes the risk out of making the wrong decision. If you decide to retire, take a year and travel, and then realize you're bored out of your mind, you can find a job. Your portfolio might be a little smaller, but that won't matter anymore.

This is the one section in the book where I can say that I haven't accomplished it yet. Becoming a millionaire at age 28 was a great milestone, but I haven't won the financial game by achieving financial independence just yet.

FIRE followers often refer to "lean FIRE" or "fat FIRE" based on your level of expenses. Lean FIRE is focused on reducing expenses to a level where a smaller portfolio can sustain it. A great demonstration of this is Mr. Money Mustache, who retired at 30 by drastically cutting expenses. For example, he ditched the idea of driving around in "clown cars" and now bikes everywhere.

Fat FIRE, on the other hand, means you can keep your clown car. Fat FIRE allows for higher expenses and, in turn, requires a bigger portfolio or other passive income. Rachel and I are pursuing fat FIRE, and not just because I've put on a few pounds lately. We hope to have a solid 50-60 years of life ahead of us that we plan to use to raise a family, travel the world, and other things that are not cheap. For example, I'm training to get my private pilot's license, which I will use to travel even more frequently. With these expensive goals ahead of us, a $1 million portfolio will not give us everything we want.

Luckily, we're not looking to retire as soon as possible. Rachel and I both enjoy having something to contribute to, and our current jobs aren't bad at providing that sense of fulfillment. Longer-term, we'll probably find something with more flexible hours, so we don't have to schedule our lives around a 9-5 commitment. Fortunately, our portfolio provides us with the means to take big pay decreases if needed to find the right fit.

By following the methods laid out in this book, I have been able to ski in the Swiss Alps, become a millionaire by age 28, and have an unlimited range of life opportunities ahead. And I was far from perfect in my execution. I hope that by sharing my successes and failures, I have helped you visualize the path to achieving your goals.

It is now up to you to execute that vision. Regardless of your current financial standing, you can take control of your finances and quickly accumulate wealth. And you don't have to be lucky to do it. You can make small life changes to optimize each element of your personal wealth equation. You can get rich and fulfill your life desires, never worrying about money again. You have everything you need to start right now.

I look forward to hearing about your journey to becoming the next millennial millionaire.

If you found this book valuable, I would greatly appreciate a 5-star review on Amazon! Just pull up your orders page, find this book, and click "Write a product review."

Have a question or just want to fill me in on your net worth journey? Catch me on the Bogleheads forum or email me at blake@millennialmillionairebook.com

ACKNOWLEDGEMENTS

Thank you to my wife, Rachel, for always embracing my goals, no matter how crazy they seem. I couldn't have become a young millionaire or written this book without her support and contributions (or without her meticulous meal preparation).

Thank you to my parents, Curt and Bev, for teaching me the value of money while also reminding me money isn't everything.

Thank you to my brothers, Mitch and Jared, and my friends, Jason, Eric, Danny, Jon, Jim, and Nic, for being my beta readers and making this a much more actionable book.

RESOURCES AND ADDITIONAL READING

General personal finance/life

- The Bogleheads forum, in my opinion the best financial forum on the internet: bogleheads.org
- The Bogleheads wiki, an aggregation of personal finance and investing knowledge: bogleheads.org/wiki
- Mental Health America, a resource to help find mental health professionals and maintain your mental health: mhanational.org
- The White Coat Investor, a very useful blog and forum for high-income professionals: whitecoatinvestor.com

Income

- Reddit's resumes subreddit, a community to help you improve your resume: reddit.com/r/resumes
- The Muse, a resource for all things jobs and careers, including advice on switching jobs: themuse.com
- The Small Business Administration website, for help navigating starting your own business: sba.gov
- Tim Ferris's book *The 4-Hour Workweek*

Expenses

- Research paper "If Money Doesn't Make You Happy Then You Probably Aren't Spending It Right" by Elizabeth Dunn, Daniel Gilbert, and Timothy Wilson

- Wolfram Alpha, an online calculator with detailed cost-of-living comparisons (plus thousands of other things): wolframalpha.com
- Smart Asset income tax calculator: smartasset.com/taxes/income-taxes
- You Need A Budget (YNAB), a comprehensive budgeting platform: youneedabudget.com
- New York Times rent vs. buy calculator: nytimes.com/interactive/2014/upshot/buy-rent-calculator.html
- The Points Guy, the top resource on credit card rewards: thepointsguy.com

Investing and financial independence

- *The Bogleheads' Guide to Investing* book
- Portfolio Visualizer, a website to compare historical returns of custom input portfolios: portfoliovisualizer.com
- FIRECalc financial independence and retirement calculator: firecalc.com
- Early Retirement Now, a blog with great research on early retirement strategies: earlyretirementnow.com
- Financially Alert, a blog giving advice and complete transparency on FIRE with a family: financiallyalert.com
- Think Save Retire, a blog that delves into the mindset of financial independence and provides the steps to get there: thinksaveretire.com
- Physician on FIRE, a blog to help physicians and other high-income, high-debt professionals reach FIRE quickly: physicianonfire.com

www.ingramcontent.com/pod-product-compliance
Lightning Source LLC
Chambersburg PA
CBHW052350220526
45465CB00003BA/1039